Stealing Fire

Memoir of a Boyhood in the Shadow of
Atomic Espionage

Stealing Fire

Memoir of a Boyhood in the Shadow of Atomic Espionage

Boria Sax, Ph.D.

DECALOGUE BOOKS
Mount Vernon, New York

Published in the United States by

DECALOGUE BOOKS
7 North MacQuesten Parkway
Mount Vernon, NY 10550
www.decaloguebooks.com
(914) 664-5930

Library of Congress Cataloging-in-Publication Data

Sax, Boria
Stealing Fire: Memoir of a Boyhood in the Shadow of Atomic Espionage
by Boria Sax
p. cm.
Includes index.
ISBN: 978-0-915474-13-4 (softcover)
ISBN: 978-0-915474-16-5 (hardcover)
1. Atomic Espionage. 2. Atomic Bomb. 3. Boria Sax. 4. Saville Sax.
5. Theodore Hall.

Cover and interior design by Rita Lascaro
First Edition—June 2014

*For my wife, Linda, who has given me support
in good times and bad, and who has helped me
enormously to get through the trials and tribulations
recorded here.*

*For my late mother, Susan, whose youthful idealism
gave way to stoic perseverance, in circumstances
where just getting by was no small accomplishment.*

*This book is mostly about my father. How can I
include him here? And how can I leave him out?
To the brilliance and generosity he at times showed,
and to all the splendid things that, had circumstances
been otherwise, he might have become.*

Contents

Acknowledgments

This book makes use of many previously unpublished materials, including, most significantly, writings of my father and newly declassified FBI files. I have also learned much from family, relatives, and friends. Most especially, I am indebted to my late mother, Susan; my sister, Sarah; and my brother, Joshua, for providing information and insight about my father and his espionage. I also thank my wife, Linda, as well as many friends, for their emotional support.

My thanks also go to the late Arnold Kramash, a renowned expert on espionage, and Athan Theoharis, an authority on the FBI. Both read sections of this manuscript when it was a work in progress, and offered their recommendations. I didn't always agree with them, and am solely responsible for the opinions in this book.

Then there is William Brandon, my publisher, who edited the manuscript, assisted by Michael Skakun and the Reverend Matthew S. Borden. In addition, I thank my agent, Dianne Littwin of Lit Enterprises, for all her help. She has been remarkably gracious, loyal, and persistent through all the difficulties of bringing this book to publication. Special thanks also go to Rita Lascaro, who designed this book. Her professionalism and aesthetic judgment were instrumental in bringing the publication to fruition.

When possible, I have attempted to check information by consulting multiple sources. To avoid causing embarrassment to those still alive, I have left out several personal reminiscences and changed a few names. I have included notes only for citations from books, periodicals, and other publicly available sources. Quotations and information from FBI files, as well as other personal files and communications, are identified in the text.

Publisher's Introduction

On Thursday, July 8, 2010, nine Russians and one Peruvian, all living in the United States, were arrested on charges of "money laundering" and being "unregistered foreign agents." Each of them, upon pleading guilty to a single count of conspiracy, was permitted to leave the country during the following two weeks. Within 24 hours of their pleas, they were all flown to Vienna where they were picked up by a Russian plane. They were exchanged for four Russians who had been serving lengthy sentences in Siberia for passing secret information to agents of the United States.

The children of these spies in America, who were deported with them, will face daunting psychological challenges as they endeavor to comprehend their abrupt displacement to a foreign country, as well as the knowledge that so much in their lives was simply part of an elaborate pretense. In spite of vast differences with respect to the time and political circumstances, these adjustments have some resemblance to those that confronted the Sax family. Boria Sax addresses the motivations behind the espionage and its consequences for his family and friends. In addition to being an absorbing memoir, the book is also a record of a historical era and its abiding legacy.

As I look back on several incidents from my own past during that period, I am impressed by how large a role the proverbial "Big Brother" was playing. I, too, spent most of my teenage years in Chicago, and, like Boria Sax, a few years later, attended the University of Chicago. Most especially, I recall my initial encounter with the FBI. I was on the staff of the *Chicago Maroon*, the University of Chicago student newspaper where Richard Ward was then the Managing Editor. Along with the editors of several other student newspapers around the country, Ward had at the time visited the Soviet Union as that country's guest for three weeks, and, while he was away, I had rented his apartment, an arrangement that brought me to the attention of the FBI. The Bureau contacted me, then barely seventeen years old, to meet with two of its agents in downtown Chicago. Both interrogated me about Ward's political beliefs and the reasons for his trip. Based upon positions that Ward had taken at editorial meetings of the student newspaper, I had no doubt that he leaned towards the left, but I had absolutely no idea whatsoever as to whether he was an active member of any particular political organizations. When I subsequently told him about my session with the FBI and asked him about his political affiliation, he described himself as a Communist but with a "small 'c.'"

That would have placed Ward in the same category as some distinguished personalities—Jean-Paul Sartre, André Gide, Arthur Miller, Richard Wright, and Paul Robeson. But by the 1950s, growing awareness of the mass murders committed under Stalin was discrediting Soviet Communism even among American "fellow travelers." And what was also becoming increasingly evident, which was especially troubling to me, was how little it took for someone to end up with a dossier stashed away in a government file in Washington, which could subsequently besmirch one's reputation. In my case, it was merely by renting a room for a short period. At the height of his power, Senator Joseph McCarthy had the ability to ruin reputations and careers on the basis of evidence as flimsy as that.

Although never even remotely associated with anything related to espionage, I could nonetheless sense a fear pervading the entire society, extending even to my parents who never in their lives had done anything illegal. Some months after that encounter with the FBI, I had met a young woman on the University of Chicago campus, a fellow student, whose step-father was Morton Sobell, a spy for the Soviets who was convicted along with the Rosenbergs and sentenced to thirty years in prison. We met by chance at a talk by Julian Wexley, who had just authored a book that argued that the Rosenbergs were innocent. I remarked that I thought the Rosenbergs had committed espionage, and she did not agree, but that didn't stop us from getting together on several occasions. We were both from New York and agreed to see one another there after the end of the school term.

Shortly after returning home, I received a call at my parents' home from Sobell's step-daughter. My mother, who had picked up the phone, asked me, out of curiosity, who the young woman was, and I casually mentioned her name, as well as that of her step-father, and that we were going to be getting together later that week. Soon, to my pleasant surprise, my father approached and offered to pay for the trip if I wanted to go back to Chicago for the summer. I had been pleading in vain to do so, but it was something my parents could ill-afford. What surely must have changed their minds was a concern that I was getting involved with the "wrong people," though they never openly discussed that with me. They obviously wanted to head off any potential problem that could cause. As my father used to say, "Don't trouble trouble unless trouble troubles you."

These incidents, along with several others involving government surveillance during the late 1950s and early 1960s, were enough to impress upon me just how prevalent the atmostphere of paranoia was. They also enable me to appreciate the danger Boria Sax and his family, who had a lot more reason to avoid potentially compromising situations, must have felt during that time.

William Brandon
June 2014

Introduction by Arnold Kramash

It is dispiriting to learn, in later years, that a friend has betrayed one's self and country. It is much more devastating when that person is a parent. Such it was for the children of Ethel and Julius Rosenberg. Such it was for Boria Sax, whose father, Saville Sax was revealed to be an atomic spy, along with Theodore Alvin Hall. They did much more damage to United States security than the Rosenbergs did. Although I did not know Saville Sax, Ted Hall was a friend. Thus, I felt empathy for Boria, whose perceptive memoir about his father also illuminates the mind of a spy, one who was a colleague in the wartime Los Alamos atomic bomb project.

As Harvard students, Saville and Ted fell under the spell of Marxist mysticism, which, they came to believe held a mission for them. They believed that atomic secrets, which in themselves were regarded with a certain awe, should be shared with the Soviet "utopia." When I visited Hall in exile at Cambridge University not long before his death in 1999, he was still captive to the myth and unrepentant about his actions. Saville also struggled, but his fate held different consequences. Perhaps it is no accident that his son, Boria, was drawn to the study of mythology, in which he has become a recognized author and authority. How a son coped with the realization that his father had been captive to a dangerous myth is essential reading for anyone seeking to understand spies' motivations and the disastrous emotional "fallout" upon families.

Arnold Kramish (1924–2010)
February 2004
Author of *The Griffin: The Greatest Untold Espionage Story of World War II*

And let me speak to the yet unknowing world
How these things came about. So shall you hear
Of carnal, bloody, and unnatural acts,
Of accidental judgments, casual slaughters,
Of deaths put on by cunning and forced cause,
And, in this upshot, purposes mistook
Fallen on the inventors' heads. All this can I
Truly deliver.

—SHAKESPEARE, *HAMLET* (V, II)

Author's Preface

After first learning that my father had passed secret information about nuclear weapons to the Soviet Union, I found myself compulsively reliving old memories. Things that once seemed unfathomable mysteries suddenly began to make sense. But to arrange the fragmentary memories into a coherent narrative has been a considerable challenge for me, as it is, I believe, for almost any memoirist.

Another difficulty was to let go of many of the habits acquired in scholarly work. I have cut out a lot of historical speculation and ethical analysis from earlier drafts, because so much abstract discussion simply did not seem appropriate. Notes and explanations have been kept to a minimum. To put this a bit differently, I have tried to discard any pretense of being a detached historian and write unabashedly as a participant in events.

Most difficult of all, I have sometimes agonized about what tone to adopt. The reader should not take my satiric touches for frivolity. Looking back, the events often seem both sadder and at times funnier than I can ever hope to convey.

I have recorded all events to the best of my ability. My comments about the motivations of people in this book other than myself are, however, inevitably speculative. I have claimed a novelist's privilege to present these conjectures without noting their tentative nature.

I am distressed by the romanticizing of espionage in contemporary Anglo-American culture, whether it takes the form of gushing about James Bond or glorifying Julius and Ethel Rosenberg. Perhaps covert government action may at times be necessary, but it is very rarely, if ever, either romantic or inspiring.

In this memoir, I have attempted to depict the devastating effects that my father's career in espionage had upon our family. We, the children and spouse of a spy, stand for countless others, mostly unknown, who, through no doing of their own, become caught in the intrigues of great powers.

Boria Sax
June 2014

*He had two lives: one, open, seen and known by all,
who cared to know, full of relative truth and relative
falsehood, exactly like the lives of his friends and
acquaintances; and another life running its course in
secret. And through some strange, perhaps accidental,
conjunction of circumstances, everything that was
essential, of interest and of value to him, everything
of which he was sincere and did not deceive himself,
everything that made the kernal of his life, was hidden
from other people.*

    —ANTON CHEKHOV,
      THE LADY WITH THE LITTLE DOG

If you want to keep a secret, you must hide it from yourself.

—GEORGE ORWELL, *1984*

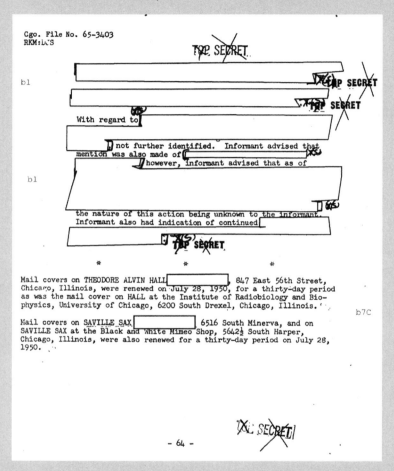

THE $64,000 QUESTION—
"WHAT'S MISSING FROM PAGE 64?"

Typical page from the FBI file of Theodore Hall and Saville Sax, where the censor has left only a few enticing hints as to its original content. The FBI must have thought the information very important, since the words "Top Secret" are not simply placed at the top of the page, as is usual, but throughout the document. The numbers and letters in the margin are an FBI code used to give reasons for the deletions.

For the Lord thy God is a devouring fire . . .

—*DEUTERONOMY* 4:24
(JEWISH PUBLICATION SOCIETY OF AMERICA, 1917)

I. Voices Out of the Past

I felt mildly annoyed at first when the ringing telephone disrupted an otherwise pleasant spring day in 1995. As soon as I picked up the receiver, the voice on the other end began speaking with an excessively precise intonation. I felt impatient, and was ready to cut the conversation short.

It was a reporter from *The Washington Post*. Without wasting any time, he informed me that my father had passed secrets about how to construct an atomic bomb to the Soviets.

Momentarily shaken, I quickly regained my composure and replied, "Well, I had not known that, but I'm not terribly surprised. . . . For some time, I have suspected something of the sort."

The reporter's voice became a bit more animated, and we had a civilized conversation about espionage.

But, when the talking ended and I had put down the phone, I suddenly felt a terrible weariness. For several months to come, I would, time and again, recall my father with alternating spells of anger, guilt, pity, fear, and frustration.

Once in the early 1970s, nearly two and a half decades earlier, my father, Saville Sax—or "Savy," as he was known by family and friends—had bragged to me about having smuggled atomic secrets.

He said that they had been given to him by a physicist named Ted Hall, but I dismissed that as a joke or a crazy boast. The turbulence of the late 1960s, when I was approaching adulthood, had spawned so many bizarre social, political, and religious movements that even claiming to have passed secrets of the atomic bomb did not seem terribly remarkable to me at the time.

Nevertheless, I distinctly remembered his mentioning Ted Hall. Over ten years later, I had quietly begun to consider whether, perhaps, Savy might actually have been telling me the truth. After my father's declaration had been confirmed by the reporter, I started to wonder whether deep down I had always known what he had done. Had I unconsciously been blocking that awareness from my mind? I recalled the air raid drills in my elementary school, when, at the teacher's directions, we placed our heads in our arms and leaned against the wall. Such memories merged in my imagination with a fear of beatings by my father, alienation from schoolmates, and all the other anxieties that filled my early childhood.

I gave away a few old magazines from my father's high school days, not wanting to have anything around that would remind me of him. But then I began to talk, little by little, about my father and his espionage, at first only with Linda, my wife, and later on with an ever-widening circle of acquaintances. To my surprise, I found that nobody held my father's espionage against me. Most people were, in fact, prepared to view him with more sympathy than I was. Eventually, the opportunity to talk about this with a few journalists—particularly Joseph Albright, the co-author of *Bombshell*[1]—was therapeutic.

Very gradually, my distress at learning about the atomic espionage gave way to relief. Many aspects of my childhood had once seemed unfathomable, almost like an inexorable curse, but now I began to make sense of them. I came to understand why my parents had been so strangely preoccupied with things like which mailing lists they might be on. I realized why, during my early childhood, we were constantly changing apartments, usually within Chicago's Black and Puerto Rican slums. I knew why my parents did not want my name in the newspapers. Above all, I learned a reason for my father's bouts of violent rage and suicidal depression—he had constantly been tailed by the FBI.

My father had dropped out of college, Harvard, at the age of twenty, and then drifted from one menial job to another. His friend Ted Hall, a precocious young physicist also studying there, had received an invitation to work on a secret project at Los Alamos, New Mexico. Upon hearing of this, my father exclaimed something like, "If it's a weapon, give it to the Russians."[2] It was. . . , and they did. My father was the courier, bringing secret information from Ted Hall to the Soviet Consulate in New York. Full of boyish ambition, the two friends had begun their careers in the sordid world of espionage. At the time, the American Communist Party, which reflected the views of the Soviet Union, imposed a military discipline among the upper echelons of its membership but relaxed control among followers on the periphery. For Savy and Ted, who became Party members, it offered a refuge from the pressures of work and school, and a forum for passionate discussions that often lasted far into the night.

The exact nature and importance of the information that the two young friends passed to the Soviet Union is not, and may never be, entirely clear. The authors of *Bombshell* believed that Hall had been a more important spy than even senior scientist Klaus Fuchs, but no other scholars support that claim. According to popular opinion, there had been some sort of "secret" of the atomic bomb, but all of the science that went into it had been publicly available before production of the bomb began. The Manhattan Project produced no scientific breakthroughs. What it did produce was a mass of technical detail about the manufacture of the bomb, which, despite its great importance, only made sense in the context of the entire production

THE BIRTHPLACE OF THE ATOMIC BOMB

This is the area known as the "Hill," which became one of the most highly developed parts of the site known as "Los Alamos" in southern New Mexico, where the atomic bomb was developed in the early 1940s. It was chosen by J. Robert Oppenheimer because he already owned property nearby. Today it is still one of the United States' major weapons research facilities, employing over 9,000 people.

Courtesy of the Los Alamos National Laboratory Archives

process. So as to avoid investing in a method of construction that might not work, the Soviet Union tried to confirm information by obtaining it from more than one independent source. It is possible that Hall did little more than corroborate the data already provided by Fuchs, but this alone would have been no small contribution to the Soviet bomb.

After the bombings of Hiroshima and Nagasaki in 1945, a time when most scientists were leaving Los Alamos, Hall stayed on to study with the physicist Edward Teller, known today as the "father of the hydrogen bomb." Even at the start of the Manhattan Project, Teller had declined to work on the atomic bomb in order to concentrate on bigger things. Hall followed Teller to the University of Chicago to work on the hydrogen bomb, only abandoning this study when he failed to obtain a security clearance in 1946. The physicist Arnold Kramash has related to me that Teller, who hadn't been aware that

Photograph by unidentified East German photographer

KLAUS FUCHS (1911–1988)

Hans Bethe, a Nobel Prize Laureate in Physics, reportedly called Klaus Fuchs, "the only physicist I know who truly changed history." Fuchs, despite both his brilliant intellect and turbulent life, comes across as an oddly passive figure, whose personality does not seem commensurate with his historical importance. After receiving a doctorate in physics in England, Fuchs returned to his native Germany and joined the German Communist Party in 1933, the same year that Hitler rose to power. Fuchs then went into hiding for several months, and managed to escape to England. He worked on the Manhattan Project, where he became the senior British scientist, while passing secret information to the Soviet Union. When accused of espionage, Fuchs initially denied the charge but later confessed. He did not seem to appreciate its seriousness, and expected that his contrition, together with providing information that led to the successful prosecution of his courier, Harry Gold, would lead to a suspended sentence. He was condemned to fourteen years in prison, of which he served nine, and upon release resumed his career as a physicist in East Germany. He may then have helped the Chinese develop their nuclear bomb.

Hall was no longer authorized to work on atomic weapons, continued to share information with him even after the clearance was rescinded. While Hall never acknowledged this, I think it almost certain that he, and probably my father as well, also played a role in passing on secret information about the hydrogen bomb to the Soviets.

Bombshell by Albright and Kunstel, the book that first chronicled their espionage, was based primarily upon extensive interviews the authors had conducted with Ted Hall and his wife, Joan. When the book appeared, Joan Hall bought numerous copies, which she then proudly distributed to all of her friends. The Halls come across in *Bombshell* as a typical young couple of the period—painting their apartment, struggling through graduate school, and starting out on careers. They appear quite ordinary, sometimes to the point of blandness, and accounts of my father's eccentricity are interspersed to provide a few comic interludes.

At times, the Halls' accounts remind me of situation comedies on television from the 1950s. None of the personalities seem entirely real, and their acts of espionage often come across as little more than adolescent pranks. But the darkness of this little domestic drama surfaces occasionally in unguarded statements by the Halls. Recalling Truman's announcement of the first Soviet atomic test, for instance, Joan Hall remarked, "I was really proud of him [Ted]. It was as though he had done it all by himself."[3]

The only living person I knew of who might have been able to corroborate the accounts in *Bombshell*, was my mother, Susan. After my father had left her in the late 1960s, she remarried, moved to Arizona, studied anthropology, and organized festivals for the Arizona State Historical Society. Upon retirement from her career as a librarian, she had worked as a counselor in a shelter for the homeless. Finally, after the death of her second husband, she had a passionate affair during her seventies, the great love of her life, which ended with the abrupt death of her new partner.

When I questioned my mother about that era, she observed, "It seems like another life." She would talk about it only haltingly, revealing hardly more than one detail at a time. Her manner, however, betrayed little tension. It was as though she doubted that there was anything much about those years, bomb or no bomb, worth remembering.

In the late 1990s, I received a written invitation from Joan Hall to exchange letters. My anger was temporarily overpowered by a combination of curiosity and pity, and I hoped that she might illuminate some of the mystery in which, so it seemed to me, my parents and grandparents had lived. Joan was educated and sensitive, but I gradually came to realize that any real dialogue with her would be impossible.

When she was pressed, the thoughtful intellectual vanished, and I would be confronted with the loyal Communist. She saw herself and Ted Hall as innocent victims of persecution. When I asked her about the over 20 million killed by Stalin, whom she and her husband had supported, she responded, "So what? Don't you realize that Capitalism is destroying the world?" She then added that, in any case, she and her husband had known nothing about those murders at the time.

After an excerpt from *Bombshell* had appeared as an article in *The New York Times Magazine*, I responded with the following letter, written with the help of my wife, Linda, and which appeared in that publication on October 5, 1997:

> In "The Boy Who Gave Away the Bomb" (by Joseph Albright and Marcia Kunstel, Sept. 14, 1997), the physicist Theodore Hall justifies passing atomic secrets to the Russians by himself and my late father, Saville Sax, with the presumed consequences of an American monopoly of atomic weapons. This argument has an eerily technocratic ring. It reminds me of the argument used to justify the bombing of Hiroshima and Nagasaki: that this allegedly kept the bomb from being used again for over half a century.
>
> While I believe Hall is sincere in his reconstruction of the past, I am skeptical as to whether maintaining the balance of terror was the actual reason for the passing of information. Recounted after more than 50 years, it may well reflect a combination of rationalization and forgetfulness. My suspicion is

that belief in the Marxist utopia may have been a greater factor than we are led to think.

At any rate, it is distressingly easy to see how these two naïve, idealistic young men might be caught up in the sweep of circumstances far beyond their capacity to control or even comprehend. But even when many extenuating circumstances are factored in, they still gave the deadliest weapon the world had ever known to one of the most brutal regimes in history.[4]

I had struggled to make the statement as balanced and restrained as possible, but not everybody understood it that way.

At her request, I met Joan Hall, in New York City a year or so later. She assured me that her husband had nothing to do with passing material on the hydrogen bomb to the Russians. I didn't believe her, but said little in response. Then she told me, no doubt having my letter to *The New York Times* in mind, "You can have your conservative views, but when you tell somebody that you know more about his reasons for doing things than he does himself, that is terribly insulting. . . ."

"We had better stop right there," I replied in an excessively controlled tone of voice, "or else I will start saying things that I don't want to say." I felt startled, and even a little bit frightened, by the anger that was welling up within me.

"I suppose you're right," Joan responded, "we have hardly any time together, and it is not possible to deal with such things now." We spent most of the next hour sharing relatively innocuous, yet bittersweet, reminiscences.

Afterwards, I wrote to Joan and her husband, who was then still alive, that when you do something as serious as atomic espionage, "everything, including your motives, becomes subject to scrutiny." When Ted Hall died about a year later, in 2000, I sent his wife a note of condolence, but there was no further communication between us.

Ted Hall was far less loquacious than his wife, and probably not as articulate. The closest thing to an explanation he ever gave for passing atomic secrets to the Soviet Union is a statement at the end of *Bombshell.* The United States could have suffered another Great Depression, he argued, in which case the country might have turned Fascist, and maybe it would then have dropped an atomic bomb on China.[5] Stripped of equivocations, this justification is just a tangle of dubious scenarios for what "might have" transpired had the Russians not been able to produce atomic weapons so soon.

It is very easy to construct events that "could have happened," and, since history is so utterly unpredictable, nobody can ever prove that one is wrong. There are those who argue, for instance, that the United States actually saved millions of Japanese lives by bombing Hiroshima and Nagasaki, thus quickly bringing World War II to an end. Alternative histories can be, and have been, invented to rationalize the deeds of every mass murderer from Attila and Genghis Khan to Stalin, Hitler, and Saddam Hussein.

Hall said absolutely nothing about loyalties, beliefs, or values that could have inspired him to pass atomic secrets to the Soviet Union. One might have expected him to make a deathbed confession, in an effort to make his peace with the world. On the other hand, if he really felt unjustly persecuted, he could have made a far more determined effort to argue his case. Instead, he evaded responsibility by offering, in place of an explanation, only a short piece of historical fiction.

Part of the reason for this avoidance was that, after a lifetime of practicing concealment to avoid prosecution, Hall was unable to break his habits of reticence and duplicity. He spoke of his younger self, the man who passed atomic secrets, as one might speak of a naughty child whom one cannot control, understand, or disown.

Two years after writing his statement for the authors of *Bombshell,* Hall died of cancer.

In 1999, I contacted the FBI, requesting their file on my father. Nearly a year later, when I had almost forgotten about it, I finally received a phone call from an FBI representative.

She graciously explained to me that they had two dossiers on my father, which together amounted to over 2,500 pages of material. To declassify the entire file would take more than five years. If, however, I would modify my request and be content with approximately 750 pages, which the FBI judged the most significant and important ones, the request for information could be processed within six months.

Why, I wondered, did releasing the files need to be so complicated? After all, it was over half a century since my father's acts of espionage had taken place. By the time I spoke with this FBI representative, not only Theodore Hall and my father but also almost everybody else who had been involved was dead. Any interest in the case was, or at least should have been, historical rather than strategic. But I didn't feel like agonizing over their reasons for the delays and readily amended my application.

Over a year passed, and still no files arrived. Despite repeated phone calls to the FBI, I received only bureaucratic assurances that my request under the Freedom of Information Act was being processed. Finally, I wrote to the FBI again, and within a week the files, a repository of forbidden knowledge, like that of the nuclear bomb itself, were in my mailbox.

I felt like a child lying in bed and listening to a violent argument going on in the next room. Ought I really to be reading such material? Was I trespassing? Few people have ever been able to come as close to revisiting their childhoods as I did by going through those papers from the FBI. Odd phrases preserved in the files evoked long buried, at times painful, memories, which are far too private for me to ever explain. As I read the files, I was torn between anger at and sympathy towards my father.

I had entered an eerie world of subterfuge, a parallel dimension accompanying everyday life yet seldom intersecting with it, like the world of spirits in traditional lore. Almost every document was stamped "secret" or "top secret," and had entire sentences, at least names, blocked out. Often, a page was hardly more than a collection of black lines, with only an enticing phrase or two still readable.

The techniques used to investigate my father listed in an FBI memo dated June 1, 1950 included, among other things, going through his trash, reviewing all transactions in his bank account, and reading his mail. The memo also states that the FBI "will determine the daily activities, contacts, and associations of Hall and Sax," a euphemistic way of saying that the FBI was following the two young men around. According to this same memo, the FBI also intended to "contact Illinois Bell Telephone Company." Most ominously, the FBI was looking into "the possibility of utilizing highly confidential investigative techniques."

What I found particularly disconcerting was the detached style of these reports, as if the agents were scientists chronicling the lives of laboratory animals. There are no expressions of anger, frustration, affection, triumph, or humor—nothing that might humanize either Savy, Hall, or themselves. The files contain vast amounts of factual material but virtually no analysis, which is probably part of the reason why the Bureau proved so inept at investigating the case.

At times I wonder what was going on behind the grave expressions of these fellows in trench coats and fedoras, who surely must have had their own trials and tribulations. According to one memo, dated March 16, 1951, two agents were tailing my father in a car, when one of them got out and followed him on foot. Two thugs approached their vehicle and threatened the remaining agent, but a voice on the two-way radio—at the time, a technological novelty—startled them. The assailants immediately fled, firing a pistol, though nobody was killed or even wounded. For the G-men, as for Ted Hall and my father, concealment was not simply a pragmatic option—it had become a way of life.

My mother confirmed that in the late 1940s and early 1950s, ill-concealed agents, dressed as business executives, were regularly posted outside our home. They trailed my father throughout the city, and their constant presence may well have cost him several jobs. Strange clicks on our telephone indicated that it was being tapped. Quite a bit of information is attributed in the FBI files to a "confidential informant of known reliability," in other words an undercover agent. It would have been hard for my father to complain about this, being a spy himself, but it surely complicated his relationships with friends and colleagues. He could never know whether a stranger, or maybe even an apparent friend, might be working undercover for the FBI.

The FBI "interviewed" all "known acquaintances" of my father. In addition to obtaining information, this was a way of sending a message—'This guy is trouble; keep away from him." The Bureau was conducting psychological warfare against an unstable, mentally vulnerable human being. Even when the investigation was finally discontinued, my father still spoke, in a paranoid fashion, of people following him on the streets.

One of the entries in the FBI file, dated December 12, 1954, shows just how much racial segregation was taken for granted in Chicago. It reports that Savy was hired as an elementary school teacher and that his boss ". . . considers the subject entirely too liberal because he fraternizes too much and too closely with the students' parents, both White and Negro." The name of the boss is withheld, but the document notes that he "further states that because of this persistent action on SAX's part. . . ." After that ominous beginning, the rest of the sentence is crossed out.

Despite, or perhaps because of, the limitations of the FBI, its files may be among the most illuminating records of that historical period. The documents are filled with seemingly random details, the paraphernalia of everyday life, which are so often fascinating to historians. Most especially, such files provide a record of the things that people, whether agents or subjects of investigation, wanted either to discover or to hide.

Why, for example, did the FBI take, so far as I can tell, no notes at all about the layout of my parents' apartment yet make an exhaustive inventory of the books in their library? I can't help feeling some nostalgia for the days when everyone, even hard-boiled FBI agents, felt that books had such great importance.

A land of wheat and barley, and vines and fig trees, and pomegranates;
A land of olive-trees and honey.
A land wherein thou shalt eat bread without scarceness,
thou shalt not lack any thing in it;
A land whose stones are iron, and out of whose hills thou mayst dig brass.

—*DEUTERONOMY* 8:8-9
(JEWISH PUBLICATION SOCIETY OF AMERICA, 1917)

II. The Matriarch

I still occasionally daydream about my grandmother's Russian village. Grown up, I find myself strangely drawn to conservative, small towns, places that might once have made my parents, strangely sheltered in the big city, nervous indeed. I love to explore out of the way shops and to wander down country roads. And what is it I am looking for? The "real" America? The village of my grandmother? Or perhaps the idyllic childhood I never had?

My grandparents on my father's side came from a nameless village near Vinnitsa in what is now Ukraine, connected to the larger world by means of a dirt road, a carriage house, and four horses. I know full well that many aspects of their lives there were anything but idyllic. My grandmother, Bluma, told of having to hide in a basement during Easter and Christmas, as drunken young men wandered about looking for Jews to beat up. Nevertheless, that village became idealized in family lore as a place, apart from the Ukrainian thugs, of innocence and holy simplicity, which blended into the communist utopia.

To many in the United States, the Communist Party appeared to be daringly bohemian, its utopia a more exotic and glamorous version of the American dream. The iconic image of the Communist utopia was a prosperous peasant and his wife, holding shovel and pitchfork as they gazed ecstatically into the future. The image of the American Dream was a house in the suburbs with a smooth lawn, a car, and children playing. But, apart from matters of style, these two visions of the future were not very far apart.

The Czarist regime in Russia had confined Jews to Ukraine, and they could not leave even temporarily, much less move, unless they received special permission. Meanwhile, the Czarist government also oppressed Ukrainians, and used a "divide and conquer" strategy with the two groups. When there were unpopular policies, the government would blame Ukrainians to Jews, and Jews to Ukrainians. When the Bolsheviks took power, Jews were disproportionally represented in their ranks. But when Stalin broke with Trotsky, it created a split among Jewish Bolsheviks, with my ancestors siding with Stalin. In 1932–33, there was a minor rebellion in Ukraine, and Stalin ordered all grain to be shipped out of Ukraine, creating a famine in which about seven million died, mostly from starvation.[6] Then in the Moscow trials of 1938, Stalin turned on all of the old Bolsheviks, especially Jewish ones, while still honoring Lenin and the Revolution. In the last year or so of his life, Stalin, always paranoid, became preoccupied with an alleged plot of Jewish doctors to poison him and was planning a massive pogrom that his death in 1953 cut short. Bluma and some of her friends, however, continued to venerate him even after that.

When it comes to these events, I certainly don't go around saying, "Never forget!" They make a pretty depressing story, where villains are many and heroes are mostly lost to history. I would be happy to consign this period to a very well-deserved oblivion. What I feel is not exactly anger and not exactly hurt, but an overwhelming sadness. If I speak of it with a touch of humor, as I sometimes do in this book, mostly out of a feeling that, in confrontation with the terrors of history, humor seems to be all that I have left.

Once they had arrived in America, my grandparents and their friends, many from the same village, recreated their Jewish ghetto in New York City. They all moved into the same apartment building, got together every day, and regarded the rest of the city, indeed American society, as heartless and corrupt.

Courtesy of the author

Saville Sax, with his sister, Ann.

In silvery photographs of my father and his family from the 1920s through the 1940s, the grown-ups appear immaculately dressed and very deliberately posed. They have grave, dignified expressions, as though they already thought of themselves as living in an exalted past. The only spontaneity comes from the children in those photos, who are obviously having a hard time keeping still. This was long before the instant snapshot was invented, when being photographed was still a time-consuming, momentous, and expensive undertaking.

According to family members, my grandfather arrived in the United States in the spring of 1914 together with his future wife, just before the outbreak of World War I. He had come to work in his father's shop as an upholsterer. Searching the archives of Ellis Island, I found only a single immigrant whose profile even remotely resembled that of my grandfather. A certain "Boruch Saks" of "Russian-Hebrew" nationality had arrived from "Weksina, Russia" on March 6, 1914 aboard a ship from Bremen called the *Scharnhorst*. He had only two dollars on his person and was planning to join his father, Isaac Saks, in New York.

The spelling "Saks" was sometimes used for our family name, and "Boruch," which means "blessed" in Hebrew, could easily have been used as a variant of "Boria" or "Bernard"; "Weksina" was roughly equivalent to Vennitsa, perhaps misheard by an immigration officer who didn't understand Russian. Boruch Saks was 17 at the time of passage, just the age my grandfather would have been; he was also five feet four inches tall, about the same height as my grandfather.

The only puzzle is that Boruch Saks is listed as having blond hair, while my grandfather's was dark. Could it be that my grandfather had, for some reason, bleached his hair or worn a wig as a disguise? Could he have been a fugitive? Maybe even a spy?

As for my grandmother, I have been unable to find any record whatsoever of her arrival at Ellis Island, despite days of searching through ship manifests, in which I also looked for many variants of her name. Could she, perhaps, have been somehow smuggled into the United States?

Upon first coming to America, my grandfather delivered newspapers; Bluma, my grandmother, made lace and sold it on the street, pretending not to speak any English until a potential buyer offered an acceptable price. After a while, my grandfather opened his own upholsterer's shop, but kept it for only two or three years.

The Bolshevik coup of 1917 provided the family not only with an identity as Communists but also a generous income. In desperate need of cash, the new Russian government began selling treasures looted from Czarist palaces at a fraction of their true value. My grandfather saw his chance and began importing these for the American market. He quickly prospered, without the need to make any real accommodation to his new society. I suspect him of having converted to Communism, mostly because it was good for business. He lived what we call "the American Dream," but that ideal had merged in his imagination with the Communist utopia.

My grandfather remained a Russian citizen during and even after the Bolshevik rise to power; he was not naturalized until November of 1920. Everyone in his circle adored him, especially the women. People said that he could look at a garment without taking any measurements, immediately start cutting, and duplicate it exactly.

For all his Communism, my grandfather was a rather typical entrepreneur of the early twentieth century—energetic, adaptable, charismatic, and occasionally ruthless. In a self-portrait that he painted, as well as a few old photographs, he has the rounded cheeks, receding chin, and furrowed brow of my father, while his large, nervous eyes show considerable tension. Just gazing at this stern, if troubled, patriarch, I feel a little intimidated.

Bluma, my grandmother, and her husband were gradually followed to America by her entire clan, which formed the core of a tight, little Russian-Jewish community: her father, Jacob Chikovsky, known affectionately as "Dyadya," full of colorful stories; her sister Haika, along with her brothers, Abraham and Moishe, all arrived in the United States in 1919. Their best friends, Jacob and Sonia Ostrowsky, also came from the same village as my grandparents and shared in their veneration of Stalin. Though Sonia had adopted Jacob's family name, the couple derided marriage as "bourgeois" and would not consecrate their union with even a civil ceremony.

Jacob Ostrowsky died before I was born, but his wife Sonia, a tiny, wizened woman, was a familiar figure. She couldn't abide even casual criticism of either Stalin or Russia, but, since she never looked at a newspaper, she didn't seem to realize that Russia had deStalinized well over a decade earlier. She used to walk up to Hasidic Jews and declare indignantly, "I can hardly believe that in the twentieth century you still dress in such an antiquated manner!"

A revolution was actually about the last thing that the people in the circle of my grandparents, worn out by anti-Semitism in the new world as well as the old, really wanted. Communism served one purpose for them—to provide cohesion in an apostate Jewish community, as a halfway house between orthodoxy and secularism. The trouble was that the accommodation worked too well, leaving the community cut off not only from gentiles but also from many of their fellow Jews.

Even during my early childhood, my grandmother seemed about as ancient as a person could possibly be. Although Bluma was only in her fifties or sixties, she already had long white hair, which, when unbound, extended down almost to her knees. Her short stature, barely five feet, gave her a gnome-like appearance. The wrinkles in her face, though few, were deep, and her eyes a pale grey. At times she boasted about days when her eyes had been blue and her hair blond, not realizing that these features seemed to betray what, for her, may have been a distressing secret. She had been raised by a domineering Polish stepmother, whom she never ceased to resent. For all her claim to be a pure-blooded Jew, she herself may have been partly Polish.

My grandmother appeared to have no aspirations beyond being a dutiful wife and mother, but she, nevertheless, had such a strong will that she terrified her children and grandchildren. As one of the renters at her country place once put it, "Her favorite activity seemed to be what she called 'telling my tenants vot's vot.'" She was indignant that many people thought Russian Jews didn't farm, and was always ready to offer advice about raising vegetables.

But she adamantly refused to adapt to her new country, even neglecting to learn how to use public transportation. Bluma hardly ever went out of her West Side apartment in Manhattan except to go shopping at the supermarket just around the corner. When occasionally she was forced to go further away, usually for a medical emergency, she would either get a ride from a friend or take a taxi. She always shouted whenever she used the telephone, louder if it was a long-distance call.

Bluma conflated Communism and Jewishness so completely that she almost lost the ability to distinguish between the two. Except for Chanukah, neither Savy nor Bluma ever celebrated a single Jewish holiday. Even the Jewish festival of lights was only observed occasionally and rather half-heartedly, perhaps as a lesser evil that was indulged in to keep the kids from celebrating Christmas. My grandmother was

GRANDMOTHER

Four miles to the nearest shop or town,
A single mile to the nearest farm,
Grandmother owns a ragged plot of land
And no-one knows exactly where it starts.
There was barbed wire there when I was small,
Behind it was a field of geese and cows.
The wire has disappeared. The field is overgrown.
A few trees are cut down, but yet the cottages
Have only lost some paint in all those years.
They needed a coat then—and need it still.

She was as old as anyone could be,
Or so we thought, but she is older now.
Her husband, son and daughter all are dead.
One grandchild has died. The rest are grown.
A neighbor painted her, a gnarled branch in hand,
The long white hair bound up upon her head,
The trees above her, taller every year.
She walked the path she's walked so many times.
When she too dies, then all of this will change;
Weeds overwhelm the paths her feet have worn.

A Russian village was her only home.
She never felt at ease upon these shores
With autos, bank accounts, insurance, bills,
Policemen shouting, planes, and neon signs
(No more am I, but somehow I get by).
She always shouted on the telephone.
It may be she still plots against the Tsar,
But he is dead. And she will die as well.
The rooms that she has lived in fifty years
Will fall into decay or else be sold.
 —Boria Sax, 1983

Courtesy of the author

Courtesy of the author

Bluma Sax in front of a portrait of her (not shown in full) by Sarah Sax.

Published in *The Raven and the Sun: Poems and Stories* by Boria Sax, (Providence: The Poet's Press, 2010) 35–36.

about as scornful of Orthodox Jews as she was of Christians, yet she felt her Jewish identity was unassailable. Paradoxically, the rejection of religion brought, perhaps in compensation, an intensified sense of Jewish exceptionalism.

Not long after starting his import business, my grandfather purchased 150 acres in upstate New York for about $600, and built a bungalow colony. This might seem a pretty big indulgence for a Communist, but I doubt my grandfather looked at it that way. To the outside world, the bungalows were a status symbol, and they established him as the unchallenged patriarch of his little community. He saw them as a sort of utopian community, a re-creation of the ghetto without the poverty or threats, a Jewish enclave in a gentile world or—what seemed almost the same thing—a socialist enclave amid capitalism. He had become a little Moses or Lenin, and the bungalows housed his new society.

Exactly how did my grandfather manage to amass money so quickly? Plenty of other importers had more capital, more connections, and more experience, but perhaps he was more discreet. He seems to have kept entirely aloof from the turbulent strikes and other political activities that rocked the garment industry during the 1920s and 1930s, which may have been so as to avoid public notice. At one point, he opened a bank account in an assumed name, which could have something to do with personal intrigues or business dealings as well as politics.

My grandparents and their friends took pride in having the most "progressive" views, but the women in their circle were absolutely subordinate to the men, far more so than in American society. The women would go off and talk about housework, while the men talked in a very abstract, dreamy sort of way about revolution, and everybody appeared fully satisfied with that arrangement.

My grandfather became a sophisticated world-traveler, while Bluma remained a simple peasant woman, whether from preference or lack of opportunities. She unwittingly made herself less attractive to him simply by following his precepts as a Communist. The Marxists scorned anything traditionally feminine as "bourgeois decadence." My grandmother never wore makeup or paid attention to clothes; she turned herself into an icon of peasant virtue, worthy to adorn a poster in the style of socialist realism, but received little gratitude.

According to several of the women in their circle, my grandfather once even intended to leave his wife, by taking her on a trip to Russia and then ditching her, so that he could return home alone and set up housekeeping with his mistress, the niece of Jacob and Sonia Ostrowsky. All of the arrangements were in place, but he suddenly lost his nerve. For one thing, his heart condition had been taking an inevitable toll. In his will, my grandfather acknowledged having an illegitimate child, no doubt the product of his liaison with the Ostrowskys' niece, and directed Jacob Ostrowsky to serve as the infant's guardian.

Still, some of my fondest childhood memories are of people in my grandparents' community sitting around a bonfire at my grandmother's country place long after my usual bedtime, with a huge samovar, brought over from the old country, filled with boiling tea. We children would throw old bottles and bits of broken glass into the hottest part of the fire. Such evenings, as I remember them, did not seem to end with sleep but simply faded into the next day, when I would get up quickly and hurry out to see how the glass had melted. Those times, however, seemed to hold out a promise that would never be, and could not be, fulfilled, and that makes the troubles to come later still more poignant.

For all their supposed radicalism, the community around my grandparents was traditional enough to practice an arranged marriage. This was actually no longer habitual even among them, but it was the revival of a long-abandoned tradition of the *shtetl*. What made it possible for the family to resuscitate such an anachronism was the isolation of their tiny circle from the norms and expectations of the larger society.

My grandfather picked out a husband for my Aunt Ann, my father's sister, the most tragic figure in our profoundly troubled family. Her long, flowing locks and large eyes, so gentle and delicate, made just about everyone love her instantly. Hyman Arenberg, the chosen bridegroom, was a man close to my grandfather's age, who met almost every qualification in his eyes. He was rich, Jewish, and a doctor, though one of the few people in this community to remain highly skeptical of Communism.

You could hardly have found a better exemplar of the American Dream than Arenberg. He had come to the United States as an orphan at the age of 12, but with a little help from the Russian-Jewish community, had managed to work his way through medical school and to establish a moderately successful practice. Sadly, however, he had allowed himself little or no time for intellectual exploration or social experimentation. He knew very little beyond medicine and his tiny enclave of fellow immigrants. While ready for some well-earned relaxation and family life, he did not know how to find or court a girl.

At the time, Ann had a boyfriend of her own age whom she hoped to marry. Bluma, my grandmother, for the first and only time, defied her husband to side with her daughter. My grandfather, however, soon became very ill and died. His last words were his wish that his daughter marry Arenberg, and everyone in the family felt obligated to honor this final request. After the marriage had taken place, the ill-matched couple seemed to do little together except fight.

Arenberg, though little interested in either religion or ideology, nevertheless shared the old-fashioned ways of his community. Ann, very skilled in crafts, wished to make and sell hats, mostly just for the creative activity. Her husband forbade this, however, saying that no wife of his would work for her living. She accepted his veto, though under protest. As consolation, Ann took full advantage of what amenities her position allowed by parading around in expensive furs and flashy jewelry.

Ann and Arenberg had one child, Barard. Like my father, Barard was torn between the Russian-Jewish community of his birth, which he knew intimately, and the American mainstream, so full of promise yet still so unknown. He grew up to be a large, gregarious young man, cracking jokes incessantly, though more out of nervousness than merriment. People often remarked upon his keen intelligence, but Barard realized that success in American society would require venturing beyond the Russian-Jewish ghetto in which he had been raised.

The community held its young people with an enormous power, since they had been taught to fear the outside world, an America supposedly filled with covert Nazis. Young men in the Russian-Jewish ghetto were constantly pampered, flattered, and fussed over, yet they floundered on their elders' ambivalence toward America. They were given mixed messages, pushed intensely, even brutally, towards academic and professional accomplishment, yet also urged to despise the rewards of success.

People within the enclave valued potential in young men, so much so that they would be disappointed by any genuine achievement. The only way out was to "beat the system"—to succeed by either sheer brilliance or trickery, getting good grades without studying, or making money without working steadily. That could not be kept up for long, so many of them ended up as janitors or chess bums.

Barard's first attempt to enter the mainstream came when he went to college and moved into an apartment with some buddies. Ann insisted on coming over periodically to clean up after him, to Barard's immense embarrassment. Within a year, he had flunked out of college and returned home, but his second attempt to escape the ghetto was more serious.

Barard committed the ultimate act of rebellion—he married a young woman from outside his community. She happened to be Black, but, far more significantly, she was a gentile. Bluma, Ann, and Arenberg, nevertheless, all seemed to accept her, if a bit grudgingly. At least she wasn't Polish or Ukrainian! Instead of appreciating their valiant attempt at liberalism, however, Barard worried that his point was being missed. He began flaunting his wife, kissing her loudly and caressing her flamboyantly in front of his relatives. Juanetta, for that was her name, knew that her husband genuinely loved her, yet she surely could not help feeling a bit exploited. The marriage eventually broke up, and then Barard blew his brains out with a revolver.

Ann and Arenberg achieved a sort of intimacy in the end, perhaps not the closeness of lovers, or even of friends, so much as that of old enemies, people who have been fighting one another for so long that they eventually develop a mutual respect. Ann, eventually, became terminally ill with breast cancer, and asked Arenberg to give her a lethal injection. She stipulated only that, without telling her, he should pick the moment of her death. A few years after fulfilling her request, her husband died of old age.

Bluma became the honored matriarch of her community upon her husband's death, and, though once feared, she ever so slowly became beloved. Whether out of stubbornness or integrity, she had clung to her odd notions of propriety. She was an icon, a relic from an earlier, perhaps simpler and more blessed, age.

"You are not one hundredth of the man my husband was...," she had once told my sister's drunken boyfriend, "and you never will be." But those who had known her for a long time realized that even her bursts of temper, terrifying though they might seem, were usually brief. And, in her last decade—she was to die in 1986—the old gruffness gradually fell away, revealing a gentleness in her that nobody had suspected. She, who had seldom smiled before, began to do so all the time, and even aches or pains could only temporarily impede her cheerfulness.

Bluma outlived her husband, both her children, and one grandchild. While she excused her husband for having given up their daughter in marriage, she never forgave Arenberg for accepting his offer. In the year or so before her death, her mental powers failed to the point where she was frequently unable even to remember family names, but she still would not gaze at a picture of Arenberg without cursing him.

Having grown up speaking Yiddish and Russian, Bluma learned English, her third language, only after immigrating to America. In her final years, she sometimes forgot her English almost completely and reverted to a blend of the tongues she had learned as a child. I knew just enough of those languages to be able, at times, to get the drift of what she was saying.

Bluma would recount, more to herself than to me, disconnected memories, mostly from her childhood in Russia, which gained increasing vividness as the decades that followed them faded into oblivion. She talked about her elementary school, where she had received good grades in Russian but not in Hebrew. She spoke with undiminished fury about two "Polish girls" who used to pick on her, and she had plainly not forgiven Poland for producing them. The independent union Solidarity was then leading a rebellion against Soviet rule, but she told me never to support it because, "Hitler was the king of Poland."

Having attained prosperity without needing to make any accommodation with American society, my Russian grandparents left Savy with all their psychological problems of adjustment to America but few of their economic opportunities. Not much was left financially, for just about all of the Czarist treasures had been sold.

Savy had hardly any sense of the inner logic that holds society together, and saw American culture as a puzzle in which every detail had to be figured out. He could often startle people with surprising insights, yet these would only come in transitory flashes of inspiration. From the start, Savy had been torn among three radically different cultures: the medieval traditions of the ghetto, the revolutionary heritage of his community, and the bourgeois ethos of America. He and his family were, in consequence, doomed to a period of downward social mobility.

I will not cease from mental fight,
    Nor shall my sword rest in my hand,
Till we have built Jerusalem
    In England's green and pleasant land.

—WILLIAM BLAKE, *MILTON*

III. Old Ways in the New World

Savy's mother, following a custom from her homeland, had begun to toilet train him almost as soon as he was born. She did this by tying him to the potty with a rope, and would not release him until he had gone. She made no attempt to teach him to eat properly until he was six years old, preferring to spoon-feed Savy and avoid any unnecessary mess. Though both of Savy's parents knew English, they spoke only Yiddish to him until the day came for him to go to school.

Their other old-world customs included having Savy share a room with his older sister well into adolescence, which might have been necessary in the cramped quarters of the Russian-Jewish ghetto but not in their New York apartment. His parents had two living rooms, one of which could easily have been outfitted as a bedroom for one of their children. To compound his problems, Savy was discouraged from adjusting to the American way of life. Things like infrequent baths, a hardship that couldn't be avoided in a Russian village, became a point of pride in his new country, distinguishing his people from the American bourgeoisie.

A scrap from a journal Savy kept as an adolescent states, "My goal is to create a world revolution. It must come soon. My sister is driving me crazy with her nagging about the housework." He aspired to be another Lenin, in much the same way that other kids at the time dreamed of becoming Babe Ruth or Joe Louis.

A few weeks after a vehement argument with his father, Savy, then twelve years old, was entrusted with administering heart medicine to his father at specified times. But one day, the young man fell asleep, and failed to perform his duty. When, shortly afterwards, a heart attack killed Bernard, Bluma placed the blame on her son. Savy, carrying an enormous burden of guilt about his father, even named me after Bernard (using his nickname) as an attempt at expiation. Savy's guilty conscience gave Bluma enormous emotional power over him, and his only chance to get out from under the parental shadow seemed to be by some transcendent accomplishment.

My father, like many in his Russian-Jewish community, regarded those outside their circle with suspicion, while simultaneously feeling drawn to the vast, enticing, and terrifying world that is America. With only a vague notion of the mores and expectations of American society, he had no idea how people do such basic things as getting up early each morning to go to work, let alone building a marriage or a career.

Language difficulties and social alienation made Savy an indifferent pupil in grammar school, but he blossomed briefly at DeWitt Clinton High School in the Bronx, where he formed a literary group with his close friends, Emile Capouya, later a highly respected critic and translator, and James Baldwin, the famous novelist. Despite difficulties with English, Savy was fully able to hold his own among these gifted companions. He could make up for what he lacked in grammar through passion, imagination, and grand ambition.

The advisor of the literary circle was a young teacher by the name of Dorothy Lyon. I don't know just what her relationship with

Courtesy of the United States Postal Service

JAMES BALDWIN (1924–1989)

Following a long tradition of American writers that included Ernest Hemingway, Ezra Pound, and Allen Ginsberg, James Baldwin moved to Paris in 1948. In addition to literary companionship, he sought greater acceptance as both a Black and a homosexual than he was able to find in the United States. In the latter 1950s and 1960s, he received great acclaim for combining the cosmopolitan intellectual traditions of the great European capitals with a focus on Black America. He appeared on the cover of the May 17, 1963 issue of *Time*, and was considered a leading candidate for the Nobel Prize for Literature. He aligned himself with the more militant branch of the Civil Rights Movement, represented by the Congress on Racial Equality (CORE) and the Student Nonviolent Coordinating Committee (SNCC), and was also attracted to the Black Nationalism of Malcolm X. By the end of the 1960s, he ceased to be a social activist, though he continued to publish prolifically until his death.

Savy may have been, but he later thought of her far more as a girlfriend than an authority figure. In that romantic era, teachers as well as students were attracted by his disheveled appearance, intense eyes, and racial ambiguity.

Our family was probably descended in part from the Khazars, a Turkish people from Central Asia that converted to Judaism in the early Middle Ages, which might explain the dark complexion that enabled Savy to accompany Baldwin to Harlem and pass for Black. One reference in Baldwin's memoir *The Fire Next Time* almost certainly refers to my father:

> *My best friend in high school was a Jew. He came to our house once, and afterward my father asked, as he asked about everyone, "Is he a Christian?"— by which he meant "Is he saved?" I really do not know whether my answer came out of innocence or venom, but I said coldly, "No, he's Jewish." My father slammed me across the face with his great palm, and in that moment everything flooded back—all the hatred and all the fear, and the depth of a merciless resolve to kill my father rather than allow my father to kill me and I knew that all those sermons and tears and all that repentance and rejoicing had changed nothing.*[7]

Baldwin goes on to tell his father, "He's a better Christian than you are," something that Savy would certainly not have taken as a compliment.

In any case, Savy later believed Baldwin had exploited him much in the way a Renaissance prince might have used his Jewish banker, constantly borrowing money for fancy clothes and expensive restaurants with no intention of paying it back. The resentment may also have been due to jealousy, but Savy, at any rate, did not read Baldwin's books and seldom spoke of him.

Savy had repeatedly attempted to enlist in the military but was rejected for service because the fingers on his left hand were stunted, a deformity more psychologically troubling than physically limiting.

Once, during his childhood, when other kids had made fun of his hand, Savy picked up an axe in rage and ran after them.

In place of military service, he tried to participate in the war effort by working in a defense plant, Atlantic Metal Products in Long Island City, but his mother showed up there and insisted that he quit. My own mother attributed this to class snobbery—the idea that manual labor was beneath the Sax family. Today, I strongly suspect that Bluma may have taken her son out of the factory because she was setting up a liaison for him with the Russian government. He had confided to her his desire to pass the secret weapon to the Russians, and she had arranged for a suitable opportunity. At first she directed him to Earl Browder, head of the Communist Party in the United States, and later to a contact in the Soviet Consulate. Bluma's leads may have been provided by relatives still in Russia, whom she contacted through Russian War Relief, an agency set up to provide assistance for her devastated homeland.

I can well imagine that contributing to the war effort may have given my father some consolation for the pain of rejection by the armed forces. His modest role as a manual worker perhaps made it easier for him to submerge personal ambition in the larger task of victory in the war. And by helping the American war effort, he also indirectly assisted the Soviet Union. This mission gave meaning to what must otherwise have been an excruciatingly monotonous routine. It also introduced him to a broad spectrum of American society, cutting across barriers of ethnicity, age, class, and education.

I recall my father occasionally saying nostalgically that he would have liked to start life over as a manual laborer. As a child, I just thought this wish was like wanting to play policeman. As a young adult, I thought it was a Marxist sort of bucolic sentimentality. Much later, I realized that he had probably been expressing a very explicit wish that he had remained at work in the defense plant rather than engaging in espionage. Shortly afterward, when he had become a foreign agent, participation in normal life would be impossible for him.

I doubt that my grandmother reflected much upon her involvement in atomic espionage. She had a chance to help her beloved

Photograph by Henry Waxman

EARL RUSSELL BROWDER (1891–1973)
Chairman of the Communist Party of the United States

Earl Browder had the sort of turbulent career typical of many Socialist radicals during the early to mid-twentieth century. It included repeated prison terms for agitation and espionage, editing radical newspapers, running twice for President, and writing several books. All the while, he was intensely engaged in the internal politics of the Socialist movement, which was marked by many shifting alliances and splits. He became head of the Communist Party of the United States in 1932, but then upset the Soviets in 1944 by stating Communism and Capitalism could peacefully co-exist. The Soviet Union, which wanted to assert greater authority over its foreign representatives, had Browder removed from office in 1945 and expelled from the CPUSA the following year.

Russia, which had suffered so much in the war, and that was all she needed to know. It probably never crossed her mind that she might be engaging in treason, betrayal, or anything of the kind.

In the mid-to-late 1940s, Savy and Bluma received a communication from relatives still in Russia stating that it had become too dangerous to remain in contact. Russian Jews could often get into a lot of trouble with the Soviet government for corresponding with relatives abroad, but in this case the contacts had been in the service of Communism. The relatives were probably more frightened about the FBI than the KGB. Had Bluma and Savy thought their relatives were seriously threatened by the Russians, they might not have continued to venerate Stalin and the Soviet Union. At any rate, family members told people that the Nazis had killed all our relatives. My father later fabricated an enquiry about Bluma's sister and brother-in-law in Russia as an excuse for associating with employees of the Soviet Consulate.[8]

Russians—be they Jewish, Christian, or Communist—seldom have an easy time adjusting to American society. Formalized contractual relationships, where duties and obligations are specified in excruciating detail, are comparatively alien to them. They are, most especially, unused to compartmentalizing their lives into personal, political, and professional realms. My father grew up in an environment that was at once stiflingly traditional and daringly bohemian, never learning the rhythms of work and relaxation that enable people to hold steady jobs. Just as the community in which he grew up was a re-creation of the Jewish ghetto, so, I believe, the ring of spies in which he worked later became a substitute family, even a sort of "utopian" community. The spy ring, like my grandparents' circle, was marked by extreme closeness and mutual dependence, and it sealed itself off from the rest of the society. Despite their frequent appeals to universal values, the morality of spies and their fellow contributors is essentially tribal, a matter of "us" versus "them," with all the intimacy and ruthlessness that carries with it. Nobody can sue or call the police if obligations aren't met, so spies of a hostile power have to look after one another.

It seems odd in retrospect that the Soviets would have taken on a spy as mentally unstable as Savy, but Savy's first handler gave him an excellent report. Savy couldn't hold a normal job because he was not comfortable in impersonal business relationships. He was highly manipulative, and more at ease negotiating the fluid relationships of loyalty, debt, and intimidation that are part and parcel of a spy network.

I have often wondered about what transpired between Savy and his Soviet handlers. These spymasters often had little understanding of American society, but made up for that lack by an almost uncanny understanding of human psychology. They knew how to identify the needs of their charges and to command loyalty. Realizing that Savy was lonely, alienated, vain, imaginative, confused, and almost endlessly vulnerable, they offered him sympathy and understanding. Above all, they granted him membership in a secret elite. But, seductive as the enticements of espionage may have been, I suspect my father might have been ready to trade them all for a simple sense of community.

Had Savy grown up a couple of generations later, some of his problems might have been relatively easily addressed. In the mid-twentieth century, however, institutions such as universities did not have nearly as many social and psychological services as today, and a far greater stigma was attached to using them. Perhaps medications now available might have alleviated his depression and rage. Tutors could have addressed his deficiency in basic academic skills. But once he had smuggled military secrets to the enemy, his social contract with American society was forever severed. He could no longer talk freely about his problems or claim the assistance that, otherwise, might have been his due.

True, all of us start to collect dreams of "What if. . . ?" by the time we reach our mid-teens. Speculations about missed opportunities often leave even conventionally successful people feeling angry and embittered as their lives draw to a close. In my father's case, such musings have special poignancy, since a single act of youthful arrogance, of perverse idealism, abruptly destroyed any prospect of either a normal career or healthy family life.

After high school, failure at Harvard, and success at espionage, Savy married a gentile and moved away from his mother, but could not find, or create, a new home. Susan, his wife and my mother, told me that he hit her even before they were married. The first blow was in public at Pinebush, my grandmother's country place. Susan had innocently made a remark that, at a time of extreme sensitivity following the Holocaust, my father interpreted as anti-Semitic. He suddenly struck her and shouted, "See what it feels like!" Part of his rage may have been genuine, but the act was undoubtedly also calculated, a signal to her as well as the others that blood family would always come first.

I can still vividly remember the time our family had gotten all dressed up one evening to see the film *My Fair Lady* at Chicago's Michael Todd Theater. This was the city's most splendid old movie palace, appointed with massive chandeliers, finely upholstered red chairs, and gilded statues along the periphery of the balcony. Together with my brother and sister, I sat in awe of the decorations as we waited for the show to begin.

Suddenly, my father exclaimed, "I just had a terrible thought!"

"What is it?" I asked.

"Suppose an atomic bomb were to fall right now," he replied. "All of these people would be shut up in the theater together. Pretty soon there would be cannibalism. . . ."

Then, to revive the festive mood, he tried to make a joke out of his remarks: "Say, I wonder who would get eaten first!"

As the movie began, horrific scenes of people in the audience literally tearing one another to pieces kept going through my mind. I glanced over at my father who seemed to be watching the film intently, but perhaps he was really lost in some reverie.

*For I, the Lord thy God am a jealous God, visiting
the iniquity of the fathers upon the children unto
the third and fourth generation....*

—*EXODUS* 20:5
(JEWISH PUBLICATION SOCIETY OF AMERICA, 1917)

IV. Why Spy?

Why did my father become a spy? Why did Ted Hall, and why, for that matter, would anybody? Well, why do alcoholics drink or gamblers play at cards? All of these addictions often begin with idealism. The thwarted idealist may turn to drink to ease his disillusionment, only to end up caring more about beer than love or politics. CIA operatives may cease to care much about democracy, and agents of the Kremlin can lose interest in Communism. Much like alcoholism, espionage fosters a very intense, if often superficial, feeling of solidarity with a group of soul-mates. Alcoholics like to imagine they are too sensitive to live in the same manner as other people; spies think they understand the world too well.

But the best analog of all for espionage is war. The philosopher Sissela Bok has pointed out in her book *Lying: Moral Choice in Public and Private Life* that the mystique of deception is very close to that of violence. Both activities are highly dangerous means of coercion that are precariously circumscribed by religious and moral codes. Both, however, are celebrated in epic poetry: violence in the person of Achilles, for example, and falsehood in that of Odysseus.[9] Violence is the center of life for the professional soldier, while falsehood is that of the spy. Both vocations offer people the opportunity to engage with impunity in such activities as killing and fraud that are otherwise socially unacceptable. Nonetheless, they are exalted in countless movies and novels, though each very often appears sordid upon closer examination. There would be few wars or none if armed conflict did not fascinate people, and there would be little espionage if people did not find spying romantic.

A mystique of secrecy, which renders spies and spy novels so alluring, pervaded almost everything about American culture in the immediate postwar decades. The Freudians believed that they could uncover hidden meaning and symbolism everywhere, from politics to dreams. The Marxists thought that they alone were privy to the covert dynamics of history. Advertisers of the mid-twentieth century constantly emphasized the "secret ingredient" in their toothpaste or the "secret recipe" for their canned spaghetti. Politicians often avoided scrutiny by claiming "secret information." In a society where so much activity was based upon the deceptions of marketing and politics, the spy had become an archetypal figure.

The period from the late 1940s to the early 1960s was only very superficially placid, despite the forced cheerfulness of beach party movies and sitcoms. America was divided into hostile camps: beat and square, left and right, religious and secular, intellectual and middlebrow. One thing that all of these groups had in common was an obsession with intrigue and betrayal. The paranoia of each was used to justify that of the rest, always adding to a spiraling fear.

People constantly whispered in frightened, excited tones about clandestine organizations such as the Mafia, CIA, KGB, FBI, Communist Party, Black Muslims, Mormons, Rockefellers, John

Birch Society, and space aliens, each credited by some with near omnipotence. Stories circulated constantly about little-known elites, furtive plots, and concealed places. Many people spent their days simply roaming the streets or hanging out in bars, largely to hear secrets. As a child, I remember overhearing stories about the intrigues of undercover agencies, tales that were too complicated to follow, let alone remember. Perhaps they were, indeed, no more intricate than what some devious minds inside the CIA really might dream up, but nobody could ever make them work according to plan.

Paranoia accompanies great power. The United States was, perhaps for the first time in history, the foremost military force in the world. This supremacy was obtained largely through the exclusive possession of the atomic bomb, at times interpreted as a sign of divine election. In the words of William L. Laurence, official journalist of the Manhattan Project, "Destiny has placed its trust in our people by providing us with the key to this hitherto tightly locked 'cosmic cabinet,' and the American people must, and will, keep this trust." [10] The bomb seemed such a wonder that everything associated with it acquired a heightened importance, and the scientists who worked on its development seemed to be godlike figures.

And this mystique was almost certain to entice an ambitious yet confused young man such as Savy. A spy cannot publicly take public credit for his deeds of espionage, but can still be proud of them. Ted Hall, a very promising young physicist, certainly needed the recognition far less than the college dropout who conspired with him. Savy, who could be genial but was always fiercely competitive, must have seen Ted's accomplishments as a challenge. Having relatively little to lose, he was willing to push ahead more boldly than his partner. Ted was always far more cautious and realistic than Savy, yet, I suspect, not terribly hard to manipulate. His intellect, almost inevitably, made him arrogant, and his overconfidence made him vulnerable; he had seldom been forced to recognize his limitations. It would probably not have been very hard for somebody in a relatively high position at the Manhattan Project, perhaps even director J. Robert Oppenheimer himself, [11] to have manipulated Hall by

Robert Oppenheimer   Ted Hall

ROBERT OPPENHEIMER (1904–1967) AND TED HALL (1925–1999)

In addition to strikingly similar facial features, Oppenheimer and Hall shared a Jewish background, personal charisma, youthful radicalism, nervous intensity, attraction to Eastern spirituality, and (though Hall was the more precocious) a reputation for intellectual brilliance. We know little about their relationship, but perhaps Hall could have reminded Oppenheimer of his own youth?

Pictured above are the Los Alamos identification badges for these two physicists. Everyone in the facility from the highest to the lowliest in the pecking order was required to display one.

---

providing him with access to atomic secrets and then intentionally "looking the other way."

Ted, Savy, and their companions would often talk about history and philosophy late into the night. And here Savy, an alluring conversationalist, had the edge over his brilliant yet taciturn comrade. Wary and secretive even among friends, Savy held back some of his conspiratorial activity from Ted. For all the experiences that they had shared, Ted and his wife, Joan, later seemed to know almost nothing about Savy. They did not realize, for example, that Yiddish rather than English had been his first language, that his relationship with his parents had been tempestuous, or even that he had been raised as a Communist.

The FBI learned of Savy's espionage through the decoded Venona documents, which were so secret that even the CIA was not informed of them until 1952. After Savy, probably with the help of Bluma and her relatives in Russia, had made contact with the Soviet Consulate, the Russians arranged for him to receive and pass on secret information from Ted Hall. One of the Venona documents, dated November 12, 1944, supports the idea that the espionage was mostly at Savy's initiative [12] rather than Hall's:

> .... He (Ted Hall) decided to hand over to BECK (Sergei N. Karnakov, the Soviet handler of Sax and Hall) a report about the CAMP (Los Alamos) and named key personnel employed on ENORMOZ (the Manhattan Project). He decided to do this on the advice of his colleague Saville SAKS, a GYMNAST (member of the Young Communist League) living in TYRE (New York). SAKS' mother is a FELLOWCOUNTRYMAN (Communist) and works for RUSSIAN WAR RELIEF. With the aim of hastening a meeting with a competent person, HALL on the following day sent a copy of the report by SAKS to the PLANT (Soviet Consulate). ALEKSEI (Soviet official Anatoli Yakolev) received SAKS.... [13]

A Venona document dated December 2, 1944 records Savy's unsuccessful efforts to contact Earl Browder, head of the Communist Party USA and codenamed HELMSMAN, at the Party's National Office in New York. The FBI had also learned of that incident from a separate source. One of its agents had infiltrated the Party and was present at the time. He informed his superiors that the office secretary, probably out of fear that Savy might be an American agent seeking to penetrate the organization, had refused the uninvited guest admission. Savy had been very persistent and made a strong impression. The Party thought the attempt to see Browder might be important and reported it to Moscow.

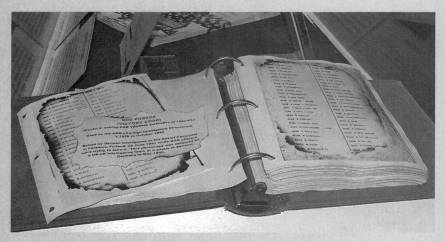

Courtesy of the Cryptological Museum of the National Security Agency, Ft. Meade, Maryland

VENONA PROJECT

Pictured above is an incomplete Soviet code book that was found on a mountainside in Finland, and then presented by Finnish officials to the American government. It is partially burned, possibly from a botched attempt by Soviet troops to destroy it during a hurried retreat. The book proved instrumental to the United States Army in decoding messages sent by Soviet officials to their colleagues and supporters in the United States. These revealed the espionage of Julius Rosenberg, Donald Mclean, Guy Burgess, Theodore Hall, Saville Sax, and many others. The messages, however, were never used in court cases. In fact, the decrypted materials were so secret that even the CIA was not made aware of them until 1952. The United States apparently did not want the Soviets to know that their code had been broken. Decoding the Soviet messages was a major initiative, involving hundreds of employees, and was known as "The Venona Project." The meaning of that name, if indeed it has one, remains a minor mystery of the Cold War.

Sergei Karnakov, the Soviet handler of the two young agents, was a former White Guard in the Russian Civil War that followed the Bolshevik coup, who had immigrated to the United States and converted to Communism. Using the cover of a journalist, he had become an agent of the Soviets. Savy and Karnakov probably shared a strong bond based upon membership in the Russian immigrant community. They could relate to one another in ways that neither Russians nor Americans really understood.

A Venona cable of January 23, 1945 shows that all was not harmonious in the spy network:

> . . . *The checking of OLD (Saville Sax) and YOUNG (Theodore Hall) we entrusted to ECHO (Bernard Schuster) a month ago, the result of a check we have not yet had. We are also checking OLD's mother. BECK (Sergei N. Karnakov) is extremely displeased over the handing over of OLD to ALEKSEI (Anatoli Yatskov, known as "Yakovlev"). He gives a favorable report of him (OLD). ALEKSEI has met OLD twice but cannot yet give a final judgment. YOUNG has been seen by no one except BECK. On the 8th January YOUNG sent a letter but never made arrangements calling for a meeting. He has been called up into the army and left to work in the CAMP (Los Alamos). OLD intends to renew his studies at Harvard University at the end of January.*[14]

While power struggles were routine among those engaged in espionage, it was unusual for the Venona documents to allude to them in such unequivocal terms.

Savy had made at least one trip to New Mexico to receive atomic secrets from Ted Hall. He had even started reading up on the American Indians in the area, so he might plausibly use the study of anthropology as a cover if anybody were to ask about the journey. The coordination of the trip, however, had been poorly prepared, and the two men nearly failed to find one another. Yatskov, who succeeded Karnakov as Savy's handler, began to notice the young man's eccentricities, and

Photograph by Ed Westcott, Official United States Army Photographer for the Manhattan Project, Courtesy of the American Museum of Science and Energy, Oak Ridge

EYES THEY HAVE BUT THEY SEE NOT

General Leslie Groves, who directed the Manhattan Project, issued strict orders that nobody was to reveal what went on at Los Alamos or at any other sites of the Manhattan Project. But, since the endeavor employed 130,000 people, that was impossible to enforce consistently. Pictured here is a billboard displayed at the Oak Ridge, Tennessee facility where plutonium was being produced for use in the bomb that would be dropped on Nagasaki.

replaced him as a courier with Lona Cohen. Savy was never one to take rejection lightly, and, coming shortly after his failure at Harvard, his removal from the case must have been shattering.

A mysterious intercepted cable from the Russians dated July 5, 1945 states that an "incident involving GRAUBER" was "a compromise of" Ted Hall. It then adds that this was due to Yatskov's "completely unsatisfactory work with the agents" at the Manhattan Project.[15] Neither Ted Hall nor Roy Glauber, (who may have been referred to, though, in that case, his name was misspelled), a former roommate of Hall at Harvard and winner of the 2005 Nobel Prize in Physics, would later admit to understanding the reference.[16]

Soviet archives reveal that, in this instance at least, Savy was spying not only on the American government but also on Ted Hall. Savy reported to his handlers that another scientist had told Hall that the atomic bomb ought to be shared with the Russians. Hall had replied that he was already taking steps in that direction, and that his colleague might do the same. The other scientist said that he had no interest in spying and, from that time on, began to avoid Hall.[17]

Savy returned to Harvard and picked physics as a major, even though he had no background in the sciences. His course of study must have been chosen in emulation of Ted Hall and, even more significantly, in hope of furthering his career as an atomic spy. He was waiting for another call to work from the Soviets, since, even had he not been intoxicated with the mystique of espionage, he could no longer return to normal life.

As Luc Santé has observed, "The atomic secret . . . ascends to the level of the sacred because it manifests in concrete form the terror that mystics can only suggest: the end of the world."[18] After his great adventure, the routines of everyday life seemed trivial to my father. Whether driving a cab or teaching grade school, he would always be "the man who passed the secret of the atomic bomb." But who could really live with this artificially heightened significance?

Like the wimpy Clark Kent, who was really Superman, Savy led a double life. To the world, he appeared as a rather slovenly manual laborer, and nobody guessed that he was really secret agent CTAR, who, though only in his early twenties, had already changed the course of history. The trouble was that his transformation, unlike that of Clark Kent, involved a great deal more than changing clothes.

. . . and Prometheus
of the intricate and twisting mind. . . .

—HESIOD, *THEOGONY*
(TRANSLATION, RICHMOND LATTIMORE)

V. The New Olympus

Prometheus, who stole the fire of Zeus from the heavens, was the first atomic spy. In *Theogony*, written about 750 BCE, Hesiod begins the story of creation with Gaia, Mother Earth, who, like my grandmother, belonged to an era that was remote almost beyond imagining. Gaia spawned the race of titans, who gave birth to the gods and who, in turn, made war upon them. According to one myth, the titans once came so close to victory that the gods fled to Egypt, where they assumed the forms of animals, but Zeus, god of the heavens, finally defeated the titans with his thunderbolts. Then the titan Prometheus, who had sided with the gods, concealed a smoldering flame from the forge of Zeus in a reed of fennel. He brought the stolen fire to humankind, and soon it was burning in every hearth.

Hesiod goes on to tell how Zeus then promised Pandora, the first woman, to Epimetheus, the foolish brother of Prometheus, in marriage. As a wedding gift, Zeus gave a box, filled with disease, death, hunger, and all the evils of the world, which was opened by the bride. Then, to punish Prometheus for the theft of fire, Zeus had him chained to a rock in the Caucus Mountains. Each day, an eagle came to eat the liver of Prometheus, who would sometimes shake the earth as he writhed in pain. During the following night, however, the liver would grow back, only to be devoured once again the next day. Finally, Hercules killed the eagle with an arrow, and Zeus set Prometheus free in return for his prophetic knowledge about the fate of the gods.

According to later versions of the story, Zeus assigned Prometheus to make Man. Prometheus felt sorry for his creation; other creatures had wings, sharp teeth, or massive strength to defend themselves, but humans seemed utterly vulnerable. Moved by pity, he gave people fire in compensation. Because of Prometheus, mankind had the use of fire, yet they remained subject to endless hardships. Prometheus was a trickster, a traitor who had first betrayed the titans and then deceived Zeus as well. Prometheus was also perhaps the first martyr, a divinity who suffered for the sake of humankind. Nevertheless, he remained a minor figure in Greek mythology, only occasionally invoked by poets or honored by priests.

Towards the end of the eighteenth century, however, Prometheus became the patron of the new spirit of scientific investigation. Goethe, Shelley and many others paid homage to him in verse. Marx called him ". . . the noblest saint and martyr in the philosophic calendar." [19] In the early twentieth century John D. Rockefeller commissioned a gilded statue of Prometheus stealing the fire of heaven to adorn the courtyard of Rockefeller Center in New York City.

Prometheus became, above all, the patron deity of the atomic bomb. William Laurence wrote of the first atomic test, "Prometheus had broken his bonds and brought a new fire down to the earth." [20] *Scientific Monthly* editorialized in September 1945 that, "Modern Prometheans have raided Mount Olympus again and have brought back for man the very thunderbolts of Zeus." [21] J. Robert Oppenheimer

Left and right above: Delaware Public Archives, Dover, Delaware

1950s CHILDREN PROTECTING THEMSELVES AGAINST ATOMIC BOMBS

Children in elementary school during the 1950s "duck and cover," placing their heads against the wall in an air-raid drill. They have been constantly told that an apocalyptic explosion, with only a few minutes warning, could come at any time. The group on the right is hiding under blankets as well for a little extra protection.

said of the atomic bomb in a speech of November 1945, "As a vast threat and a new one . . . by its novelty, its terror, its strangely Promethean quality, it has become . . . an opportunity unique and challenging." [22] A more somber interpretation, of both the myth and the atomic bomb, appeared in the issue of *Time* immediately after Japan's surrender. "Pain and a price attended progress," the anonymous author wrote. "The last great convulsion brought steam and electricity, and with them an age of confusion and mounting war. A dim folk memory had preserved the story of an even greater advance: 'the winged hound of Zeus' tearing from Prometheus' liver as the price of fire." [23] It quickly became common to refer to the creation of the atomic bomb as a "Promethean act."

The bombings of Hiroshima and Nagasaki eroded what remained of prohibitions against attacks on civilians during wartime. Even today, such acts continue to undermine the moral authority of the

United States in its struggle against terrorism. Military leaders as distinguished as General (and later President) Dwight Eisenhower, General George C. Marshall, Admiral William Leahy, and General Douglas MacArthur stated after World War II that the use of atomic weapons had not been necessary to win it. Even in the unlikely event that the United States had felt compelled to invade Japan, contemporary estimates of the likely American casualties at the time did not exceed 20,000, but our government later gave out wildly inflated figures of 500,000 American lives that had allegedly been saved.[24]

The Communist Party of the United States also enthusiastically endorsed the use of atomic bombs, and neither Ted nor Savy, so far as I know, ever expressed any regret about the devastation of Japanese cities. But the atomic bomb, as soon as it had been detonated, was regarded less as a weapon than as a talisman, a symbol of cosmic favor, whose magical aura inspired wild expectations. Factories, airplanes, and cars supposedly would soon be powered by pellets containing atomic energy, and corn grown with artificial suns. One well-publicized proposal was to melt the polar ice caps utilizing atomic energy to improve the climate. And what about global warming? No problem! Atomic energy would enable people to air-condition entire cities in the tropics.[25]

People often described this weapon in religious terms. William L. Laurence also wrote, in his usual purple prose:

> *The hills said yes and the mountains chimed in yes. It was as if the earth had spoken and the suddenly iridescent clouds and sky had joined in one affirmative answer. Atomic energy— yes! It was like the grand finale of a mighty symphony of the elements, fascinating and terrifying, uplifting and crushing, ominous, devastating, full of great promise and forebodings.*[26]

Building the atomic bomb was a holy crime, great because extreme. But a crime against what? Or whom? Surely not simply an archaic deity that people had ceased to believe in for well over a millennium.

Behind all the grand rhetoric lay guilt about the bombings of Hiroshima and Nagasaki. J. Robert Oppenheimer speaking to

Courtesy of the National Museum of the United States Air Force, Dayton

NAGASAKI, AUGUST 9, 1945
One Bomb with the Force of 21 Kilotons of TNT

This picture shows a replica of the second atomic bomb, the one dropped on Nagasaki three days after the first landed on Hiroshima, and two days after the Soviet Union had declared war on Japan. The bomb released over Hiroshima, known as the "Little Boy," had taken the lives of about 140,000 people. The Nagasaki bomb, nicknamed the "Fat Man," a possible reference to Winston Churchill, was ignited by the implosion device which the spy Theodore Hall had worked on. Though the more powerful bomb, the Fat Man killed only about half as many as the Little Boy. The Nagasaki bomb landed almost directly on top of the city's Roman Catholic Cathedral, but some distance away from the center of greatest population density.

his colleagues at the Manhattan Project after the first successful test quoted the *Bhagavad Gita*: "I am become death, destroyer of worlds,"[27] at once a confession and, even more, an arrogant boast. A weak person, who lacked firm convictions and was fascinated by power, Oppenheimer was constantly torn between pride in creating the bomb and shock at its destructive power. The scientists who worked at the Manhattan Project attempted not so much to deny as to sacralize their guilt.

If the gift of atomic power, like that of fire, was for all humanity, how could one justify hoarding it for a single nation? For those who did not think about the myth (and, probably, nobody really did), Prometheus seemed a romantic rebel. Leaders of the Manhattan Project found defiance glamorous in stories but not in real life. The complex at Los Alamos was surrounded by barbed wire. Mail was intercepted and phone lines were tapped. Even the most casual political discussions were frowned upon. Laurence reported that after President Truman's official announcement of the bombing of Hiroshima:

> It was shocking at first to hear terms such as "atomic energy," "uranium 235," "atomic bomb," come out openly on the radio. These words had been strictly taboo. They were never uttered even in a whisper. One always talked about such things in code. There were animated conversations about "barber shops" and "pigs," or we called numbers, like a quarterback calling signals, or the letters of the alphabet.[28]

Clearly, the Manhattan Project was giving spies like Klaus Fuchs and Theodore Hall plenty of training in secret codes.

Nuclear weapons, which needed to be guarded so carefully, created a culture of paranoia that quickly spread throughout American society. It should have been ridiculously obvious that, while celebrating Prometheus, the people who ran the Manhattan Project were behaving a lot more like a tyrannical Zeus. The Manhattan Project is still arguably the largest gathering of distinguished scientists in all of history. It was an Olympus, closed to ordinary mortals, where the gods of knowledge performed their wonders. For aspiring intellectuals like Savy, the Manhattan Project had all the glamour of Hollywood.

The creators of the atomic bomb had thoughtlessly shrouded their deed in an ancient myth, like a set of old clothes that did not fit, forgetting that Prometheus had been a deceiver and a thief. The real Prometheus, if there was such a person, had been an arsonist, a terrorist out to avenge his conquered tribe. Why else would he conceal a smoldering fire in his staff? Why else would he have been tortured? Prometheus, alas, had been a traitor to his people even before bringing fire to humankind, for he and his brother Epimetheus were titans who had sided with the gods.

If the new Prometheus was Ted Hall, the clever titan, my father was Epimetheus, his heedless brother. The two young men were, as imperfectly assimilated Russian Jews, strangers in the Olympus of American science. Just as scientists would uncover the secrets of nature, so others might steal those of the scientists. Ted Hall may have been a precocious physicist, but probably had no more than average political sophistication or historical perspective. In most ways, he and my father were fairly typical young men who had absorbed the rhetoric of their elders, often without full understanding, but nonetheless acted upon it more decisively than their mentors ever dared.

Prometheus' consolation, according to Aeschylus and later authors, is the clairvoyance that will earn him liberation in the end. In this final episode of the story, it was my father, not the scientists or generals, who tried to live the myth but did not succeed. During my early childhood my mother often had to support the entire family working as a waitress or cashier, since Savy was too traumatized and unbalanced to hold a job for very long. For a while he drove a taxi, during which time he was robbed at gunpoint. He held several other odd jobs, but ended up quitting or being fired for erratic behavior. Sometimes, Savy would simply walk off a job without giving notice and never go back. People who knew him wondered how such an obviously intelligent, and often charming, person could be stuck doing such pitiful work. They sensed his enormous rage, yet were enticed by his aura of mystery. He once spent weeks barricaded in his bedroom with a revolver, threatening to shoot himself if anyone called the police.

During this period, he wrote essays and verse, which he failed to publish. Despite their lack of polish, scattered phrases and lines showed a poetic gift:

> *The poet is the tip of the Universe.*
> *The penpoint of God.*[29]

Adolescent poetry filled with grand ambition, self-pity, and abstraction usually gives way, as writers learn to focus more intently on the specifics of their experience. My father's development, however, had been fixed at the time of his espionage.

Neither pen nor couch offered him much in the way of therapy. He couldn't write about his smuggling of atomic secrets, the most significant event in his life. He would not have been able to confess it, even to a therapist. To develop to full maturity, Savy would have had to confront his past, and that was, under the circumstances, impossible. It was hard for him to deal with even simple problems, such as notoriously poor hygiene, which doubtlessly kept him from those jobs that FBI surveillance had not denied him. He slapped his wife, hit his kids, and once even tortured the family dog. But he appeared to do all of these things, like his smuggling of atomic secrets, without full awareness. He always had an air of exasperating innocence about him, like a precocious yet naughty child.

The hardest thing, however, both for Savy and the rest of us in his family, was alienation from American society. True, alienation was incessantly romanticized at the time in the personas of beatniks, tramps, and others. It was celebrated in such characters as the movie star James Dean and J. D. Salinger's fictional Holden Caulfield. But what the media glamorized, however, was youthful rebellion, a mere rite of passage. My father experienced the real thing.

Communism was a fundamentalist sect in the religion of science and progress, and appealed to the mystical inclinations of both

Ted Hall and Saville Sax. Physicist and author Arnold Kramash, who worked at the Manhattan Project, told me that a colleague of his had once arranged to drop by Ted's room at Los Alamos. When he arrived, it was utterly dark, and Ted was nowhere to be seen. He looked about and found a stack of crates in a corner, on top of which Ted was sitting with his legs crossed, meditating like a Buddha.

Savy would walk through the streets in animated conversation with himself, causing people to turn and stare. He was the sort of person who in another society might have been regarded as a shaman, someone who could commune with spirits. My father vacillated between calling himself an "atheist" or an "agnostic," but he also referred to "God" in his poetry. His atheism, such as it was, was in the Jewish tradition of patriarchs like Abraham who would argue with, and sometimes reproach, Yahweh. Even the denial of God could be part of an intimate but troubled relationship.

Whatever he really thought of God, Savy's beliefs were centered far more upon man, in whose unlimited potential, epitomized perhaps by the atomic bomb, he believed. His most fundamental faith was not even in Communism but "Prometheanism"—the power of reason to bring humanity to perfection. Intoxicated with the magical power of ideas and caught up in the hallucinatory visions of Marx and Freud, he aspired to "change the world."

Savy's surviving poems make no direct, unequivocal reference to his atomic espionage, but here are some suggestive lines from one entitled, appropriately, "Life":

> *I was life like fire*
> *Changing my course*
> *With the wind and the fuel.*[30]

Did Savy mean that he was Prometheus, who, for Communists, was a symbol of proletarian revolt? Did he mean that he was the atomic blast?

For my father and his contemporaries, the bomb was a heavenly portent; for the next generation it became a terror. Children in the 1950s and early 1960s had to practice air raid drills, standing with heads against a classroom wall and imagining a pulverizing blast. Told that the bomb might fall at any moment, we watched constantly for a sudden flash of light and prepared to cover our heads. If there was advance warning, we would expect to hear a siren, and then there might be time to descend to the comparative safety of the basement. I vividly remember how, sitting at home or walking down the street, I would hear an unaccustomed noise and believe it must be "the siren." In adolescence, I thought the undercurrent of terror in our home was something like the "existential condition" of humankind that philosophers described. It turns out to have been something much simpler— the atomic bomb.

Richard Rhodes, a historian, maintains that atomic espionage actually delayed the Soviet development of nuclear weapons. The Russians, according to him, had already developed a design for an atomic bomb with twice the power and half the size of the one dropped on Nagasaki, but that Stalin did not trust his own scientists. When he received plans for the American bomb, Stalin insisted on copying them, thus losing time and money.[31] In the works of Hesiod, Prometheus is an amoral trickster, yet he was constantly invoked as the patron of the Manhattan Project. If Rhodes is correct about the Soviet atomic bomb, the clever titan made fools of all who claimed his legacy, from generals and scientists to spies, for nothing went as any of them had planned. But now atomic weapons, like the fire Prometheus first stole from Zeus, are spreading across the globe

*Split between the power of the poem and the powerlessness
of the poet in society, poets have lived the lives of spies.
They have believed they are the unacknowledged
legislators, a secret police. They have been attracted
to secret societies. . . . They have preferred to publish
anonymously or under pseudonyms. . . . They have
encoded private messages and secret formulas into their
poems. They have believed they are serving great powers:
Stalin, Mussolini, the Church. They have walked like
Charles Baudelaire in Paris, Frederico Garcia Lorca or
Charles Reznikoff in New York, invisibly through the
city, watching and listening. They have sat alone in their
rooms, imagining great plots unfolding outside.*

> —ELIOT WEINBERGER, "TINKER, TAILOR,
> POET, SPY: TALES OF LITERARY ESPIONAGE,"
> *THE NEW YORK TIMES*, OCTOBER 4, 1992

VI. David and His Goliath

Both the arts and espionage are traditionally occupations for apparent "misfits," for people who are intelligent yet have great difficulty in leading "normal" lives. A spy resembles an artist in that he must pursue his mission despite knowing that he will be misunderstood by both critics and admirers. While poets compete for fame, spies struggle to avoid notice, but both obscurity and recognition can be sources of power.

The late 1940s and 1950s was a great age of American radicalism, when many resented the restraints of law and custom. Many people expected some apocalyptic change, whether in the form of a Communist revolution, Fascist coup, or nuclear war. Just about everybody from McCarthyites to Bolsheviks sensed that the social order was very precarious, whether they thought of upheavals to come with fear or with longing. It was a time of constant expectation, of perpetual tension that could only be broken by some dramatic event. Not surprisingly, the lives of Hall and Sax were filled with long late-night conversations about politics and philosophy, with terrible fears and grandiose dreams.

Anxiety and impatience can drive some to murder, others to espionage, and still others to work for secret agencies such as the CIA. Those who make such choices enter a twilight world, apart from the laws and expectations of conventional society. The spy or agent may even feel that his words and actions have a special purity, since they do not reflect the same social codes as those of ordinary men and women. When questioned, spies usually find it surprisingly easy to deny their engagement in espionage, probably because it never seems quite real to them.

Ted and Savy became a nearly inseparable pair, united by a mystical form of Communism, their adventure in espionage, and their common heritage as Russian Jews. Both were socially awkward intellectuals living in a culture that often prizes poise, good looks, and athleticism above all else. Both took refuge from a society that seemed to have little place for them, in the abstractions of Marxist theory. Finally, both appeared fascinating to many people.

But for all their collaboration, they were not really equals. According to the standards of society, Ted was a "success" while Savy was rapidly becoming a "failure," and a pretty desperate one at that. They had entered Harvard at the same time, but Ted had done brilliantly while Savy flunked out twice. By their egalitarian ideals, these social judgments ought to have been irrelevant, yet both of them could not help but be aware of this difference. Subtle but steady pressures can erode friendships as young people are slotted into social classes, and these are as intense among political radicals as everyone else.

In the late 1940s, Ted Hall was intently considering whether or not to be open about his membership in the Communist Party. On May 30, 1948, after he had passed his doctoral exam, he wrote to Savy, "I hope that in a little while my professional position will be such that

I will be able to get away being quite open [about Communism], and I think that will be good. Until then, it would be better not to get such a widespread reputation that my professional position is endangered badly." How must this have sounded to Savy, who had no professional position, who struggled to support himself with a series of menial jobs while he tried to earn a certificate in elementary education! If one needed the status of a professional position to be openly Communist, would that mean that Savy had to refrain from activism or else sacrifice himself? Neither of the two young men, to my knowledge, ever discussed or even thought very clearly about these matters, though they did sense that their partnership was in peril. The immediate effect of the message was to make Savy take increasingly militant positions in public forums in order to show that he was not inferior to his friend.

In an odd way, however, their opposite trajectories may have temporarily drawn the two young men closer together. If success brings glamour, failure has a special romance. Though an undercurrent of tension troubled their relationship, the conspiratorial fellowship the two young people shared was, for the time being, intense enough to overpower it. Perhaps Ted had come to think of Savy as an example of the "mythic proletariat"? Savy, at any rate, must have begun to sense a patronizing note, and even a hint of exploitation, in his friend.

Ted Hall stayed on at Los Alamos long after most of the other scientists left, and then went to the University of Chicago to study under Edward Teller who was developing the hydrogen bomb. He only abandoned this study upon failing to get a security clearance in 1946, at which time Hall switched his focus to medical applications of physics. Meanwhile, Savy, readmitted to Harvard in 1945, chose to major in physics. No doubt the selection was in emulation of his friend as well as in the expectation that physics would make him a better spy. After flunking out a second time in 1946, Savy then moved to Chicago to join his fellow conspirator, probably with the intent of resuming his career as a courier of atomic secrets. He would occasionally travel from Chicago to New York in order to meet with his Soviet handlers until about 1950.

EDWARD TELLER (1908–2003), THE "FATHER OF THE HYDROGEN BOMB," VS. J. ROBERT OPPENHEIMER (1904–1967)

Which carries a bigger bang—fission or fusion? Teller opted for the latter, on the basis of ideas he had developed in conversations with Enrico Fermi during 1942. Although operating out of the Los Alamos site of the Manhattan Project, he was not directly involved with the production of the atomic bomb. Instead, he worked on creating the fusion-based hydrogen bomb, which was not perfected until after World War II.

An early rivalry between Teller and Oppenheimer turned into outright antagonism, though it is a little hard to say which of the two was the "hawk" and which the "dove." Teller spoke out against the dropping of atomic bombs on Hiroshima and Nagasaki, arguing that a high-altitude atomic explosion over Tokyo could have demonstrated the power of the new American weapon while causing little damage. Nevertheless, Teller pushed hard for creation of the more powerful hydrogen bomb, while Oppenheimer opposed it on both technical and moral grounds.

After Teller testified against Oppenheimer at Congressional hearings in 1954, Oppenheimer, then under suspicion of espionage,

lost his Security Clearance, while Teller was ostracized from the scientific community.

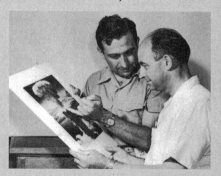

Courtesy of the Los Alamos National Laboratory Archives

Edward Teller (left) with Enrico Fermi viewing a photo of the atomic bomb exploding over Nagasaki.

Photograph by Howard E. Schrader. Courtesy of the Shelby White and Leon Levy Archives Center, Institute for Advanced Study, Princeton

J. Robert Oppenheimer (second from right) with his colleague, Albert Einstein (extreme left), on the latter's 70th birthday. The others in the photo are Gerald Maurice Clemence (extreme right), and Rudolph Walther Ladenburg (just to the right of the guest of honor).

In Chicago, Savy began a relationship with a young woman named Joan, who reciprocated some of his affection, but she soon took a liking to Ted as well. For a while, the three of them went everywhere together, pretending to be simply pals. Joan finally decided to marry Ted, leaving Savy as the odd man out. The rejection, painful by itself, harshly reminded Savy of his social inferiority to Hall.

Around 1947, just before he met my mother, Savy wrote a poetic drama entitled *David*. He gave it to me to read when I was in the seventh grade, standing over me attentively and nervously as I struggled to understand it. When I finally set the poem down, he asked me what I thought of it. Had I responded with enthusiasm or even curiosity, he might well have revealed his espionage right then. I said little or nothing, for I felt only confused.

When I found a fragment of the play in an envelope of old papers many years after Savy's death, I quickly realized that it was really about his adventures as a spy. The poem tells of a young man named Helic, representing Savy, whose father, Rosenfeld, is a predatory capitalist in Germany. Helic and his companion Charles (Ted Hall), plot the murder of Rosenfeld (espionage), with the qualified support of their friend Lolla (Joan).

The poem shows how the rivalry between Ted and Savy sometimes became pretty intense, even bitter:

Helic:	*Here comes Charles, see how happy he looks.*
	A stupid childish happiness untouched by pain,
	Childish, cruel, selfish, I'll make him suffer.
Lolla:	*Please don't.*
Helic:	*Charles, tell me, why don't you kill my father?*
	Did he not have soldiers fire on the workers?
	Was not your own brother's skull broken?
Charles:	*It is against the law.*
Helic:	*Listen carefully to what I have to say.*
	The people are enslaved by law they hate.
	He who oversteps the law by murder
	Is free and they will follow him to death.

For them he'll represent, what they would be,
Gods beyond the strength and arm of law. . . .

Charles, the sort of dithering intellectual so common in the literature of socialist realism, refuses to become a killer, but then says, "We'll do it together both together and rule the earth."

The drama continues:

Helic: *How diseased the German nation is,*
      That I must do your murders for you.
      Besides I'm leaving here to go with Lolla
      To the fearful wilderness of jungled Africa.
      Will you?
Lolla: *I suppose I will, though this is mad.*
Charles: *Congratulations.*
      Don't think you fooled me with this talk.

In a while, the three are interrupted by the distant voice of Helic's father.

Lolla and Charles leave, so Helic is left alone to ruminate on power, and then Rosenfeld appears:

Rosenfeld: *I am your father.*
Helic: *I know it.*
Rosenfeld: *I gave you life.*
Helic: *You gave me birth, you never gave me life.*
      Life I steal from heaven or from hell.
      And if I cannot live, this emptiness
      Shall be the pattern for all eternity.
Rosenfeld: *It was written long ago,*
      Thou shalt not kill.
Helic: *I deny you, I deny that.*
Rosenfeld: *Christ died to save you from the sin.*
Helic: *I care not if he dies again.*
      I kill a million years of Christs.

Rosenfeld: You cannot live without them.
Helic: Then I kill myself (He stabs Rosenfeld).

Fearing that Lolla will be horrified by his deed, Helic denies responsibility, and tells Lolla that Charles is the perpetrator. Unexpectedly,
that makes Charles into her hero, and Lolla deserts Helic for him.[32]
The play is full of common adolescent preoccupations: filial rebellion, uncertain sexual identity, and lack of direction. Savy, apparently,
thought that Ted had stolen his glory and his girl.

Engaged in the tasks of growing up, Savy had not been emotionally or intellectually prepared to cope with the enormous power that
fell his way. He wrote in a notebook that his "main intention was to
perpetuate the friendship of the three of us as the primary fact of our
lives," referring, of course, to Ted, Joan, and himself. Shortly after
being rejected by Joan, and largely to ease the tensions in his circle,
Savy married my mother. But the big news in *David* for me was that
Joan Hall had, apparently, been perhaps the great love of my father's
life. His transports had always seemed to be abstract passions about
imaginary utopias. I had previously noticed no signs of him even longing for a deeply committed relationship with another human being.

. . . our grim, guilty, tormented experiments, which were at once as chill and joyless as the Russian steppes and hotter, by far, than all the fires of Hell.

—JAMES BALDWIN, *THE FIRE NEXT TIME*

VII. Fire and Ice

My mother, Susan, was of Scottish and Irish ancestry on both sides of her family, and had grown up on Chicago's North side. Her mother, who had the richest head of red hair I have ever seen, had been baptized a Congregationalist, though she converted to Quakerism late in life. Her husband worked for the telephone company, and had been a radical socialist in his youth, though he later converted to both churchgoing and far-right politics.

The 1945 yearbook of her high school, Francis W. Parker, summed up Susan as, "extreme liberal about racial equality." The Civil Rights Movement, which was just beginning to become organized after World War II, appealed not only to her desire for justice but also for romance and adventure. It was closely associated with jazz, American expatriates in Paris, and sophisticated style.

Susan was one of only three or four founding members of the organization Congress on Racial Equality (CORE), which later achieved national prominence. CORE would eventually become a Black Nationalist organization, and later a Conservative Republican one, but its initial mission was racial integration in Chicago. It sent mixed groups of Blacks and Whites to places that had previously been patronized only by Whites, such as an ice-skating rink or a softball stadium, and the activists were sometimes met with violence. Her best friend from high school, Gail Barazani, who later became a noted artist, told how, when she and Susan had once participated in a demonstration for integration, "I was a coward; she (Susan) did not flinch. I would have fled once, but couldn't because she stood up and moved forward into the melee with people who were angry and armed with baseball bats and two-by-fours."

But Susan would later hardly ever talk about her work in the Civil Rights Movement, and, when she did, it was in a tone of resignation. She had become disillusioned, if not with the cause itself at least with her own participation. Perhaps she had found herself unable to deal with the petty infighting which, so very sadly, seems to fill almost any mass movement, no matter how noble its goals.

Cultural heritage in the United States today has become a matter of subtle nuances, and it is usually hard to tell how much of a person's avowed identity is wishful thinking and how much is real. But there is something very Scottish in my mother's combination of romanticism and practicality. The Scots had followed Bonnie Prince Charlie in a quixotic, doomed rebellion against the English in 1745, and were brutally crushed the following year. After the English had outlawed nearly everything in highland Scottish culture, from its music to its language, the Scots turned their energies to marketing and industry. They soon became renowned for thrift and pragmatism, but pursued the ideals of progress in a paradoxically melancholy way. They were also known for sad songs, strong drink, and getting into brawls.

Others would probably not have thought anything of the sort about her, but my mother was constantly troubled by the fear that

Susan and Saville Sax on their wedding day, flanked by Bluma Sax, Savy's mother, on the far right, and Winifred Healey, Susan's mother, on the far left.

Courtesy of the author

life might be passing her by. Most of the time, my mother was very sensible in her decisions, and her common sense is the major reason our family managed to survive. But there was also a repressed romantic side to her. She drank and smoked heavily; she was constantly drawn to tormented people and extreme situations. Susan lacked the self-confidence to take charge of her own life and, instead, had the dangerous habit of living vicariously through others. She admired rebelliousness, and even failure.

Before their marriage Savy told his intended bride, "I might suddenly be shot," a statement she at first dismissed as expressing only his love of melodrama. Then, gradually picking up little hints, she began to realize the reason for his fear. To marry my father was a protest against her parents, both of whom initially thought Savy was seedy and disreputable, and their bourgeois mentality.

Susan and Savy had decided to marry in 1947, when the espionage at the Manhattan Project was over, though Savy remained in contact with his Soviet handlers. My mother later told me that she had found out about Savy's service as a spy from overheard conversations between him and the Halls, but could not remember exactly what they said. Perhaps, like me much later, she did not take his claims seriously when she first heard them, and only gradually became convinced of their truth. Had Susan chosen to become a spy, she would have made a much better one than Saville or even Ted. Her native reticence would prove useful and, unlike her husband, she never told anybody about the atomic espionage.

Whether she realized it or not, my mother was in a great deal of danger. It was, and remains, a very common tactic for government authorities to find some pretext for arresting a spouse or girlfriend of a presumed agent and holding that person in effect as a hostage in order to obtain a confession. The federal authorities would soon do this with Ruth Greenglass to force her husband, David Greenglass, an atomic spy, to confess and implicate his brother-in-law, Julius Rosenberg. They would then do the same to Julius Rosenberg by threatening his wife Ethel, who had been, at most, only peripherally involved with her husband's spy ring.

Like many young men of his era who were first drawn to the glamorous vocations of art and radical politics, Savy suddenly found himself in the position of a bourgeois *pater familias*. The relationship between my parents had probably never been very harmonious, but it is hard to guess what unspoken passion underlay it. My mother and Savy both advocated a very "rationalistic" attitude toward relations between the sexes. She told her children that they ought never to allow themselves to be carried away by infatuation but should carefully consider the pros and cons of a potential mate. She talked about courtship in such detached, pragmatic terms, that it seemed to me as though she were giving directions for purchasing a television. My parents would also have said without hesitation that, of course, people in frustrating marriages should get divorced, but they didn't practice what they preached, at least not right away.

It is hard to guess how Savy would have reacted if the authorities had arrested Susan. At any rate, he never showed much gratitude for her silence. He used to strike her from time to time until one day she threatened that, if he did so once more, she would call the police. That, of course, did not mean simply intervention by a social worker or even a few weeks in jail. Any contact with law enforcement officers might have raised questions about Savy's past, which, in turn, could

DAVID GREENGLASS (1922–PRESENT)

Left and right above: National Archives, New York City

David and Ruth Greenglass.

If I am for myself alone, what am I?

David Greenglass is a good example of a fairly average man caught up in historic events that he could not control. A lens grinder with only a high school education, he entered the United States Army in 1943, where he was soon promoted to the rank of sergeant and assigned to work on the Manhattan Project in Los Alamos. He was converted first to Communism and then spying for the Soviet Union by his wife, Ruth Greenglass. Through his courier Harry Gold, Greenglass passed secrets to Soviet officials. Although not a scientist, David Greenglass understood enough to make an accurate, though not very detailed, diagram of a nuclear bomb that worked by implosion. This may well have been the first specific information about the atomic bomb to reach Soviet authorities. When exposed by the Venona documents, Greenglass, who by then had become disillusioned with Communism, implicated his sister, Ethel Rosenberg, and her husband, Julius.

Greenglass' testimony remains controversial today. Since he received the rather severe punishment of fifteen years in prison, nine of which he served, for espionage, scholars do not think he plea-bargained for a reduced sentence. He probably, however, implicated his sister and brother-in-law in an agreement with the prosecution to keep his wife from being charged. Agreeing to this deal showed a sense of loyalty, but to what extent do duties to a spouse override those to other relatives and friends? And did the repudiation of Communism mean that he was no longer bound by any loyalty to his fellow conspirators?

In his testimony, Greenglass stated that Ethel Rosenberg typed notes that her husband passed to the Soviet Union, a detail that was dramatically repeated by the prosecution at the Rosenbergs' trial. It may have been a factor in giving Ethel, who was no more than a minor figure in her husband's ring of spies, the death penalty. Greenglass later admitted that he might have been mistaken; in fact, his own wife could have done the typing. Was conjugal loyalty enough to justify this possible lie?

have led to a reopening of the investigation for espionage, in effect a possible death sentence. He stopped physically assaulting my mother, though he did continue to take out his frustrations on his children.

In the summer of 1947 Savy and Ted had started an organization called the "Farmer-Worker-Consumer Cooperative," which they announced in a letter to the Communist *Daily Worker* and the *Chicago Star*. Their plan was to build a broad coalition that would educate people about the idea of collective ownership and, thereby, prepare the public for the eventual nationalization of abusive monopolies. Savy served as acting President, but that initial meeting attracted only eight persons, none of whom decided to sign up.

A bit later, Savy and Ted together with their wives moved into the Horizon Co-op in Chicago, where they lived with other young people. This was simply an arrangement in which residents chipped in to share the rent and housework. The concept of a cooperative apartment was mildly daring at that time, since communal living suggested socialism. For most of the young people in that co-op, the arrangement was probably almost entirely practical, but for Savy, and perhaps Ted, the co-op was a utopian experiment, and they were not well-prepared for the stresses of communal life. Others in the co-op whispered that, after getting married, Susan and Savy had lost interest in associating with single people.

The Soviet handlers gave Savy and Ted a substantial financial donation for the organization, but less out of gratitude and altruism than to further their political agendas. Savy and Ted tried to persuade the members to affiliate with a union of cooperative organizations, almost certainly a front for the Soviet Union, but the members of the co-op refused. Savy was devastated, and wondered whether they had appealed too much to economic interests rather than to feelings of political solidarity.

Then Ted and Savy began to grow apart politically. Hall increasingly suspected that Russia had become decadent, while his erstwhile partner looked to the Soviet model with renewed enthusiasm. In a notebook, Savy accused Ted of embracing a Trotskyite deviation by extolling action for its own sake. This was, in the context of Soviet Communism, a very severe charge indeed, since the Party was still obsessed with rooting out Trotskyites. Ted, by then, was embarking upon a promising career in which any association with Communism was likely to prove a hindrance. Savy, however, saw their espionage as by far the greatest success of his life.

For a short time, he believed that he had invented a perpetual motion machine. This was a sort of second atomic bomb, the miracle he needed to set his life back in order, but his wife only complained that it was scratching up her table.

My father wrote the following in a journal on January 1, 1951, when he was driving a taxi and my mother was working as a waitress at the Beehive Restaurant in Chicago:

> I awoke about two o'clock, and made a plan with Sue whereby she would prepare the meal first and then I would get up. I took a bath; when I got out, only the sweet potatoes were started. I got very mad and said a few words loudly. Sue rebuked me for loud talk; I said I was sorry, but I felt she was wrong. Suddenly a feeling of great resentment surged up within me at the demand that I must continually be repressing my feelings, at Sue's coldness, and at her continuous resentment and harping attacks. . . .
> I blew up.
> "You never do anything on time; you are disorganized about meals."
> "I don't see why it is necessary to make a big meal; Boria and I have already eaten."
> "I worked all night and am hungry, and, besides, why did you promise to make the meal when you had no intention to?"
> Sue said that she would not talk to me if I yelled.
> I started to make the meal myself; she walked out and talked very sweetly to Boria. This is always her reaction to an argument. Withdrawal. And deep brooding resentment that lasts for months.

In making the salad, I threw the cut-off pieces to the ground. I threw the empty container of milk on the ground. Sue just kept on talking sweetly to Boria, while dressing him to take him out.

My father went on to complain about his wife's "neurotic crying," her "incapacity for physical affection," and her "superficiality." My father and mother were locked in a vicious circle, in which each drove the other to extremes. Her restraint provoked him to ever-greater melodrama, which she, in turn, answered with ever-greater reticence.

The next entry, dated January 9, 1951, reflects his despair, which was not news to me, and bluntness about his situation, which was a surprise:

Sue left to go to work at the Beehive; I listened to the radio and played with the cat, teasing her in a manner that bordered on cruelty. I am so weak, so cowardly, it is doubtful that I will ever be worth anything. Yet there is no harm in trying to make the best of this half-ruined life.

My father's mistreatment of my mother is almost as hard to forgive as his espionage, but I still feel the pathos in his words.

A woman who interviewed my father for the Office of Admissions at the University of Chicago, wrote down this short report:

Looks like a picture, either needs a shave or has very heavy beard. Frayed collar and dirty fingernails. Courteous, although looks peevish, but that's maybe just the shape of his face.

Nobody knew quite what to make of him. Quite a few were drawn to his aura of mystery, though others were simply perplexed or repelled. There was a coarse sensuality about him that Joan Hall would later call "very sexy" but others found repulsive. Part of what the interviewer was seeing, however, was weariness. Though only in his mid-twenties, he was already becoming worn out through all the years of concealment.

Both Savy and Ted would later deny having known about the mass murders that Stalin ordered, and claim their espionage was intended to preserve the balance of power. But in a letter written in 1948, Savy defended the Soviet Union from liberal criticisms by saying, perhaps thinking of the Moscow trials, that the "liberal ... objected to the execution of quisling elements, but he did not object to the absence of traitors during the war." Savy then continued:

The liberal tries during his period of adolescence once and for all to set up a standard of values. After two or three years of soul searching he comes up with some conclusions at the age of about nineteen. After a few years of comparatively minor modifications these conclusions will have to do him for life. Thus for all intents and purposes his moral attributes atrophy after the age of twenty-two. If the average life span is 60 then the liberal's values will be on the average a generation and one half behind the times. In Russia this peculiar inability on the part of liberals to grow and change necessitated the death of thousands of them after the revolution. This same characteristic on the part of American liberals may result in the death of three quarters of the world population in the next atomic war. Will those liberals that are left be forgiven?

Maybe those words were simply tossed off in a fit of anger and despair. One family friend later told me that Savy seemed to be "the angriest person I have ever seen."

There was perpetual tension in our family, punctuated by explosions of rage on Savy's part. Once he locked my mother in the bathroom and shoved me out of the apartment. I listened at the door as he walked around, swinging an ax and shouting. "Now I'm chopping up your grandmother's table!" he yelled, and I heard a big crash. But such fits of rage didn't last very long, and were followed by periods of contrition.

In a school art class, I once made a huge picture of a man in a frenzy, his lips tight and his eyes unnaturally wide with rage. It was placed on the wall of my classroom, together with several other tempura paintings that I had made. When the school had an open house, Savy came by to have a look. The next day the teacher asked me if the angry man in my picture was my father. When I replied that it was, she told me he had looked at all of my other pictures and commented on them pleasantly, but that he just walked by that one in total silence.

At last, my father tried to go into business for himself with a mimeograph machine. This device was a means for inexpensively duplicating papers before affordable photocopiers or word processors were available. It looked a little like an old-fashioned printing press in miniature, and it could turn out many readable if fuzzy copies. It was not uncommon, particularly in bohemian communities, for writers to use mimeograph machines to duplicate their work for distribution among friends, or even for sale at literary bookstores. My father duplicated many of his writings, a few of which have been preserved. His main business, however, turned out to be printing up the menus of restaurants announcing their daily specials. One Chicago restaurant had the motto, "No better steak anywhere." One day Savy printed this but forgot to include the word "No." Needless to say, he lost the account.

For a while Savy took courses at the University of Chicago, but he was not allowed to enroll for a degree. After that, he went on to study elementary education at Roosevelt College (now a university). There he managed to get good grades, but that school wasn't exactly Harvard, let alone Los Alamos. At one point, Savy had almost decided to drop out, but he went to Ted and Joan to seek advice, secretly hoping, I suspect, to set himself up again as a spy. To Savy's obvious disappointment, they urged him to persevere with his studies.

It is staggering to think about what strains both my parents labored under, and perhaps these partially excuse my father's lack of judgment. My father had been admitted to Harvard University at the age of 17. A short time later, he had found himself abruptly raised to the top ranks of his profession—that is, espionage—even though that was hardly the sort of thing one could put on a résumé. After that, he had experienced one failure after another. Not only had he been dismissed from Harvard, but he was replaced by more professional spies. And then he suddenly found himself trying to support a family with a menial job. My mother, for her part, had certainly aspired to more than waitressing and a marriage to an embittered taxi driver.

In the early to mid-1950s, our family was changing apartments more than three times a year. I recall people and events from those years vividly, though only in snatches—things like a long walk home from school, or how, during a Chicago winter, boys would huddle together for warmth and our teachers would pull us apart.

Oh that mine adversary had written a book.

—*JOB* 31:35 (KING JAMES TRANSLATION)

VIII. Questions and More Questions

The greatest mystery in this story of atomic espionage, for me at least, is not a question about how, or even why, my father and Ted Hall conducted espionage. It is why participants, more than half a century after these events, have continued to be so reticent about them. Savy, though he boasted more and more towards the end of his life about having committed espionage, related almost nothing beyond having passed a valise full of secrets to the Soviet Consulate in New York. Hall told a great deal about his life as a student in Chicago yet very little about his spying. A bigger puzzle still is why the FBI released no more than a small fraction of my father's file to me.

Almost everyone involved in the espionage was dead by the final years of the twentieth century, and the few who were still alive had retired. Communism has virtually disappeared outside of East Asia and Cuba, while Capitalism has begun to change almost beyond recognition. The espionage by Hall and my father had become public knowledge, so it is hard to see just why the FBI was afraid to release its complete records. Suppose the still suppressed files reveal wrongdoing by the FBI. Few if any would be shocked about events that took place over half a century ago, and there would almost certainly be no successful prosecution. It almost seems as though spies and spy catchers have conspired together to keep their shared secrets from the rest of us.

This reticence is beyond any pragmatic explanation, but makes psychological sense. All parties from spies to G-men have found it very hard to communicate their experiences to others, much less to integrate them into any semblance of what we call "normal life." Spies of all persuasions share a common culture, and generally feel more affinity with one another than they do with most of their countrymen. They are like boxers who may fight one another but still share their sport.

That is why Kim Philby, the famous mole in the British Secret Service, could talk of his vocation in a tone of casual superiority, as though the side one worked for was simply an incidental detail. It is also why British novelist Graham Greene, who had worked for the British Secret Service, could later write in an admiring introduction to Philby's memoir, "He betrayed his country, yes, perhaps he did, but who among us has not committed treason to something or someone more important than a country?"[33] If the "us" only refers to spies and their handlers, the supposition of Greene about "treason" may well be correct, but not if it also refers to other people. Like so many agents, from Philby and Greene to Robert Hanssen, Savy and his brilliant partner were infatuated with their own cleverness. They conveniently forgot that nations are not simply abstract entities but are comprised of human beings.

The case of my father and Ted Hall will always be linked with that of Julius and Ethel Rosenberg, who were tried for espionage in March of 1951. In late summer of the same year, the Rosenbergs were sentenced to death, though the conviction was appealed. The

FBI had learned of the espionage of Hall and my father, like that of the Rosenbergs, through the Venona documents. A memo from Assistant FBI Director D. M. Ladd to J. Edgar Hoover on June 2, 1950 suggested that Theodore Hall had been the agent who passed atomic secrets to Harry Gold. Soon, however, the Bureau began to realize that the culprit in that case had actually been David Greenglass, brother-in-law to Julius Rosenberg.[34] By that time, the FBI had focused most of its energy on the continuing activity of the spy ring that centered around Julius Rosenberg, and it had little interest in relatively isolated cases of espionage. That, at any rate, seems to be the most plausible explanation for the comparatively lackadaisical manner in which Hall's case was pursued. An FBI memo dated June 30, 1950 described Savy as a "known espionage agent," but apparently the bureau still did not consider investigating him a major priority.

It is debatable whether Julius Rosenberg or Theodore Hall was the more important spy. While Hall was more instrumental in supplying material on nuclear weapons, Rosenberg certainly was at the center of a far wider and more sophisticated ring. Rosenberg is mentioned far more often than Hall in the decoded Venona documents. If the FBI considered prosecutions for espionage not simply as a means of stopping spies but as an attack on the entire Communist movement, at home and abroad, it made sense for that agency to go after the most extensive network. Besides, the highly organized spy ring around Julius Rosenberg fitted preconceived notions of a "Communist plot" way better than Hall's relatively amateurish efforts.

While the idea may seem crazy to us in retrospect, many people from the late 1920s through the mid-1970s took the prospect of a proletarian revolution in the United States very seriously indeed, whether they feared or welcomed it. The Communist Party saw itself as the vanguard of an armed revolution, and its adversaries often believed that as well. The FBI did not see itself as simply defending the country against a foreign power but also as attacking domestic threats. The files that were released to me suggest that the FBI was as worried about the leftist organizations as about espionage. Those about Theodore Hall and Saville Sax are only comparatively lightly edited, while the sections that deal with FBI penetration of leftist organizations are so heavily blocked out that there is often barely a word or two left to read.

Part of the reason for this pattern of censorship was that a single man completely dominated the FBI and could easily impose his idiosyncrasies or prejudices upon the rest. J. Edgar Hoover permitted subordinates little opportunity for personal initiative. Surely there must have been times when agents were chuckling behind the scenes at the ways in which their adversaries had been misled, but their reports were written in an extremely impersonal style.

The FBI interrogated Hall, Savy, and Bluma during the spring of 1951. The records of those interrogations, contrary to what one might have expected, are among their least heavily redacted documents. They were not marked "Top Secret" but simply "Secret." It is possible, of course, that the records sent to me are incomplete. They were written down from notes taken by the investigators during the interrogations, and no recordings, as far as I know, were made. The files don't give the exact words of either G-men or suspects, and so much of the drama of the meetings does not come through. Only a few names are blotted out, and it is not very hard to see why the editing was so light. Compared with the enormous pressures that the FBI placed on such people as David Greenglass, Julius Rosenberg, and Harry Gold, the interrogations of my father and his co-conspirators were remarkably gentlemanly. The FBI did not "fail" to break either Ted or Savy; they didn't even seriously try. They never made any threats, even implicit ones, and they never hinted at what they knew. They also didn't try to draw the suspects out by using empathy or flattery. And, in contrast with the Greenglass and Rosenberg cases, they never questioned or tried to involve the wives of the suspects.

The FBI had no source of knowledge about the espionage of the two young men other than the Venona documents, and their agents were aware that anything they said to them might be reported back to the Soviets. Whatever they asked could reveal clues about their sources of information. The agents confined themselves to asking for

HARRY GOLD (1910–1972)

His biographer Allen M. Hornblum described Harry Gold (above, center) as, "a shy nebbish pulling off cloak-and-dagger capers." He began his career in espionage by passing industrial secrets of a sugar company in Pennsylvania where he worked as a chemist to the Soviets. Then he rose in the ranks, to become the courier of atomic spy Klaus Fuchs. Socially awkward, homely, and morbidly shy, Gold was the last person that most people would have suspected of espionage. Gold, however, started to drink heavily and tell fantastic tales about his escapades, in which he, a bachelor, completely invented a wife and family. When Gold was implicated by Klaus Fuchs, he in turn exposed David Greenglass's acts of espionage who then pointed the finger at Julius and Ethel Rosenberg.

National Archives at New York

Despite his cooperation with government authorities, Gold was sentenced to thirty years in prison, of which he served fourteen before being paroled.

A receipt entered into evidence against Gold that placed him in New Mexico at the time the espionage took place.

details about where the young men had been and what they had done, probably in hope that they would stumble. The conspirators, however, had been coached in advance by a Communist lawyer, who told them to "play dumb." Still, their interrogators managed to catch both young men in several contradictions. Savy and Ted realized, however, that it was only necessary in such circumstances to claim a lapse of memory about details, and so the contradictions did not discredit their stories.

Very often interrogations are a form of negotiation, and Ted Hall ended his in such a spirit. When two FBI agents approached him on March 16, 1951, the young physicist agreed to come along for questioning, and the interview was conducted with a very business-like sort of decorum. His Soviet handlers must have warned Hall that an interview might be immanent, for he showed no initial surprise. He claimed, truthfully or not, several lapses of memory, saying, for example, that he had never met Savy in New Mexico, and then later admitting that such a meeting might have taken place. For the most part, he answered questions in a very straightforward manner. Hall offered, however, to let the agents conduct a search of his home on the condition that no record be made of any "left wing literature." Should any such literature be found in his possession, Hall would have permission to destroy it, and agents would not later take "cognizance" of the material.

It is hard to guess what Hall may have been thinking when he made this bizarre proposal. If possession of left wing literature was supposed to be a crime, Hall had virtually confessed to it in any case. Since the FBI files were secret, there would have been, had the agents accepted the offer, no way to check whether they were keeping their part of the bargain. Even if they did stick to the deal, they might still have made mental notes of anything they found. But most importantly, the proposal was setting up an opportunity for continued negotiations between Hall and the agents.

More cunning, or perhaps less scrupulous, agents might well have tried to steer the conversation into politics. They could, for example, have startled Hall by empathizing and expressing left-wing opinions of their own, or perhaps they might have responded with a counter-offer. They might even have accepted Hall's offer as a means of developing their relationship with him. Instead, the agents simply refused the proposition, perhaps shutting down any chance for further communication. The agents were possibly intimidated by Hall's reputation for intellectual brilliance. The suspect agreed to return for further questions at a later date, but he probably realized that he had begun to weaken. Hall told the FBI three days after his interview that he would no longer cooperate with the investigation.

Savy was approached and interrogated on the same day as his partner by another pair of agents. When reading his interview for the first time, I felt a rush of pity for him, for he sounded utterly lost and forlorn. Savy claimed at the start of the interview that he had a very poor memory for things like names and dates, and, as though in demonstration, he gave the wrong year for his marriage. One passage in particular sounded very pathetic indeed, or, perhaps, very clever:

> SAX said he thinks he saw HALL while HALL was in New Mexico but that he does not recall that HALL was in uniform at the time. SAX said he was very depressed at the time and was living in a dream world. He said he does not know when he went to New Mexico but it was probably after the last time he flunked out of Harvard. He said his memory was very blank in this regard. He added that he only went to New Mexico to look around and he went there because TED HALL was the only person he could really rely on to get him out of his depression. He said he did not tell HALL he flunked out of Harvard and claimed this was the only occasion he was in New Mexico.

What Savy was saying here may not have been a declaration of guilt, but it was pretty close to the truth. All his life he had been subject to terrible bouts of depression, and he would respond to them in unpredictable ways. Savy was, far more even than Hall, revealing weaknesses to his interrogators, and he may possibly even have been close to confessing. The agents might possibly have drawn him out by asking about his malaise. But the agents went on to ask details about things like his bus or his hotel, most of which Savy denied remembering.

Towards the end of the interview, Savy did give what potentially might have been a very useful lead. He mentioned to the agents that his friend had worked with two "good physicists." The names of the two physicists are blocked out, but the first name was six spaces long and the second was seven. The names of (Edward) Teller and (Samuel) Allison fit, and Hall had indeed actually been working with them in Chicago. Both of those scientists, especially Teller, had been involved in creation of the hydrogen bomb. The agents might, of course, have learned that information from other sources in any case, but the record contains no indication that they thought the lead worth investigating. The files, at least those that have been released, contain no further mention of Teller. Savy agreed to a search of his house and was ready to continue the interview, but the FBI decided (at least so the record states) not to call him in again.

It is very hard to say, given the circumstances, how Savy and Ted ought really to have handled these interrogations. In passing information about the atomic bomb to the Russians, and deceiving even their friends for a supposedly greater cause, they had implicitly given abstract ideology more importance than personal considerations. By this time, I imagine, they were less concerned about politics than with protecting themselves and one another.

Bluma handled her interview by the FBI on March 20, 1951 with far greater aplomb than either her son or Hall. The FBI may have fought the two young intellectuals to a draw, but against this gruff old peasant woman they never had a chance. She denied that her son had ever tried to contact Earl Browder, head of the United States Communist Party, but then added that perhaps he might have done so as a joke. She also lied about her sister and brother-in-law in Russia, saying that they had disappeared and that Savy had contacted the Russian Consulate for word of them. She fielded a few more questions, and the FBI seems to have been readily satisfied.

Less than a month after Ted and Savy were interrogated, Julius and Ethel Rosenberg were sentenced to death. President Eisenhower refused to grant the couple clemency, and the Supreme Court declined to review their case. They were finally placed in the electric chair on June 19, 1953. While Julius died instantly, Ethel was killed only on the second attempt at electrocution. There were 10,000 people at the couple's funeral.

For decades afterward, entire communities in America took it for granted that the Rosenbergs had been innocent victims, framed by the government.[35] Since the couple had been executed for a crime so much like the one Savy and Hall committed, my father must have been especially frightened. In addition, he must have wondered whether innocent people were being executed for what he and his friend had done. Ted Hall later reported making an offer to his Soviet handler to go to American officials and say, "Don't pin it on the Rosenbergs because I was more responsible than they were."[36] The officer told Hall not to turn himself in, and the young physicist complied. But if confessing to save the Rosenbergs was really what Hall considered right, why did he not simply do it instead of asking the Russians for permission?

Ted Hall as well ceased to be active politically, and the two conspirators drifted ever further apart. In 1962 the Halls emigrated from the United States to England, after which they gradually lost all contact with my parents. Savy seldom even spoke of Ted after that, and when he did it was not with any particular affection. He also ceased to use Marxist jargon or extol Stalin. Savy may actually have handled the FBI interview with considerable presence of mind, but the experience left him traumatized. Cut off from any reference to actual events, his Communism then morphed more and more into a private fantasy world.

My mother later told me that all talk of the Rosenberg case became strictly taboo in our household. Savy collected a large pile of fantasy magazines like *Astounding Science Fiction*, and began reading through them to forget his troubles. He became so apolitical that he no longer even bothered to look at newspapers. An FBI memo in early 1953 stated that, "Since these interviews (of Sax and Hall), considerable additional investigation has been conducted, including interviews with virtually all known associates and con-tacts of both subjects." The openness with which the two associated with Communists suggested to the FBI that the two were not cur-rently involved in espionage. They behaved like people with noth-ing to hide, and, in any case, the FBI had run out of leads to pursue. An FBI memo of May 8, 1953 recommended that the case be closed, though the Bureau's interest in Savy would continue to flow and ebb until the late 1960s.

Agents continued to watch Savy from time to time, primarily in the hope that he might inadvertently lead them to a major ring of spies. In 1954 Savy was placed on the Security Index, which meant he could be barred from government employment. He would also have been subject to detention in the event of a national emergency. When Savy took a job teaching in a public elementary school in Chicago, FBI agents went to speak to his employer, probably to get him fired, only to find that he had already quit.

The FBI once again lost interest in my father for many years, only to revisit his case in 1964. The war in Vietnam was escalating, and so were the increasingly militant protests against it. Savy revived a pseudonym from his Communist years, John Oak, to write a short tract called "The Johnson Jokes," which he published privately. "What is the difference between Lyndon Johnson and a Linden Tree?" one joke began. "Answer: a Linden Tree never burned children in Vietnam." Not all opponents of the war found the jokes particularly funny, but once Savy read them in a coffee house and worked the crowd up into a frenzy.

Perhaps the FBI had taken note of the jokes, though that is not recorded in the files that have been released. At any rate, the Bureau thought that my father might be a potential assassin. An internal memo by an FBI agent dated May 12, 1964 stated that, "In view of Sax's background and questionable emotional stability he is being referred to you as an individual who might possibly represent a threat to the welfare of the President. . . ."

But the Bureau soon decided to dismiss the possibility that my father was a potential terrorist, another Lee Harvey Oswald. Still,

National Archives at New York

Julius Rosenberg

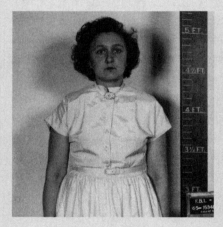

National Archives at New York

Ethel Rosenberg

JULIUS ROSENBERG (1918–1953) AND ETHEL ROSENBERG (1915–1953)

Whatever one may think of him as a person, Julius Rosenberg was a master of deception. He proclaimed his innocence so convincingly, that, for several generations, many people took it as a given that he had been framed for espionage. Typical was Jean-Paul Sartre, who told Americans, "By killing the Rosenbergs, you have quite simply tried to halt the progress of science by human sacrifice." The gradual accumulation of evidence over decades now leaves no doubt about his spying, though most scholars consider his penalty excessive.

In just about all photographs, Ethel Rosenberg appears matronly, except for a far-away look in her eyes, which suggests a poet far more than a conspirator. The consensus of scholars is that she knew of her husband's espionage, yet had at the most a very peripheral role in it. Like many housewives of the 1950s, she subordinated herself to her husband's career. She even died for it. But just what lies behind that dreamy gaze? We will probably never know.

As depicted in the Cuban postage stamp to the left, issued on the twenty-fifth anniversary of the Rosenbergs' executions, the electric chair pictured in the background is a grim reminder of their fate.

the FBI's interest in Savy revived once more in the late 1960s. The occasion was a mysterious, and heavily redacted memorandum dated February 13, 1967, based upon information obtained by the FBI from correspondence of the imprisoned Soviet spy Rudolph Abel, who went under the alias of William Fisher. That agent, who had been turned in by a drunken colleague ten years prior to the memo, had been at the center of an extensive, if not necessarily very successful, ring of spies. That, however, was just the first layer of his false identity; he was the only person I ever heard of who used spying as a cover for still more serious mischief. In fact, he was the head of a clandestine army, directed to perform acts of massive sabotage if an armed conflict between the United States and the Soviet Union were to break out.[37] The heavy redacting of the memo makes it impossible to tell exactly what the information from Abel may have been, but he appears to have asked about someone whom the FBI thought was, or at least might have been, associated with my father. The memo added that, "Extreme caution must be exercised in handling any information attributed to this source, and no action taken which could conceivably jeopardize the security of the informant or reveal his identity." The FBI then proceeded to locate Savy and Bluma. The Chicago office of the FBI initially requested permission to interview Savy a second time, but the central office of the Bureau had already decided that he was merely a harmless crank.

An FBI memo of June 28, 1967, describes Savy as an "eccentric, emotionally unstable, who lives in a dream world and is not in touch with reality." Another document, dated November 25, 1968, states, "subject is slovenly about personal hygiene and complaints have been received by the Security Office that he regularly urinates outside the classroom building rather than using the accommodations provided by the college." There was no further investigation of my father.

The conclusion that Savy did not pose a danger to the nation happened to be correct, but the agents came to it in part for the wrong reasons. Probably because they were oriented to the more conservative mores of the 1950s, they underestimated my father's capabilities. In the late 1960s and early 1970s, public tolerance for personal

A SPY FOR A SPY! VILYAM GENRIKHOVICH FISHER, ALIAS EMIL ROBERT GOLDFUS, AND RUDOLPH ABEL (1903–1971) FOR FRANCIS GARY POWERS (1929–1977)

Rudolph Abel (left) and Gary Powers (right).

Right: With permission of RIA Novewsti Archive, image #35172/Chernov/CC-BY-SA3.0

Vilyam Fisher brought a level of professionalism and dedication to spycraft that has rarely been equaled. He was born in Newcastle, England, to Bolshevik parents, who had been exiled from Russia as the result of a power struggle. Fisher was raised as a Communist, and, when his family returned to the Soviet Union in 1921, he immediately began to prepare for a career in espionage. He entered the United States in 1948 under the fake identity of Emil Robert Goldfus, complete with an elaborately fabricated biography. He directed an extensive network of spies that included Theodore Hall, Morris and Lona Cohen, and many others. In 1957 Goldfus was turned in by a drunken assistant, and immediately changed his alias to Rudolph Abel, the name by which he is best known today, in order to signal to the Soviets that he had

been caught. He received a prison sentence of 30 years.

Francis Gary Powers was a veteran of many covert aerial reconnaissance missions when his plane was shot down by Soviet anti-aircraft guns in 1956. Initially, military observers and journalists considered it amazing that aircraft flying at an altitude of over 70,000 feet could be hit by gunfire, but the mechanism that made this possible was a device known as the "proximity fuse detonator," which had initially been developed by American engineers and supplied to the Soviet Union by Julius Rosenberg.

In 1962, Vilyam Fisher was exchanged for Francis Gary Powers in a deal between the United States and the Soviet Union. Fisher then worked training agents in Russia until he died in 1971 of lung cancer. Gary Powers was killed in a helicopter accident in 1977.

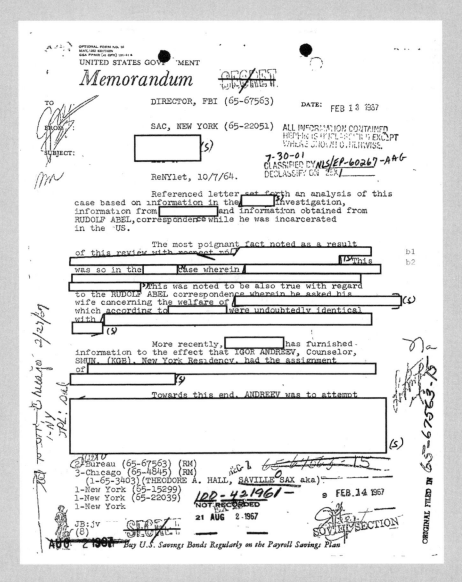

UNITED STATES GOV[ ]MENT

Memorandum   ~~SECRET~~

TO : [ ]

FROM : SAC, NEW YORK (65-22051)

SUBJECT: [ ] (S)

DIRECTOR, FBI (65-67563)   DATE: FEB 13 1967

ALL INFORMATION CONTAINED
HEREIN IS UNCLASSIFIED EXCEPT
WHERE SHOWN OTHERWISE.
7-30-01
CLASSIFIED BY NLS/EP-60267-AAG
DECLASSIFY ON 25X

ReNYlet, 10/7/64.

Referenced letter set forth an analysis of this
case based on information in the [ ] investigation,
information from [ ] and information obtained from
RUDOLF ABEL, correspondence while he was incarcerated
in the US.

The most poignant fact noted as a result
of this review with respect to [ ]   b1
was so in the [ ] case wherein [ ] This   b2
This was noted to be also true with regard
to the RUDOLF ABEL correspondence wherein he asked his
wife concerning the welfare of [ ] (S)
which according to [ ] were undoubtedly identical
with [ ] (S)

More recently, [ ] has furnished
information to the effect that IGOR ANDREEV, Counselor,
SMUN. (KGB). New York Residency, had the assignment
of [ ] (S)

Towards this end. ANDREEV was to attempt
[ ] (S)

2-Bureau (65-67563) (RM)
3-Chicago (65-4845) (RM)
  (1-65-3403)(THEODORE A. HALL, SAVILLE SAX aka)
1-New York (65-15299)
1-New York (65-22039)
1-New York
JB:jv
(8)

NOT RECORDED
21 AUG 2-1967
9 FEB 14 1967

SOVIET SECTION

FBI MEMORANDUM ON RUDOLPH ABEL

The first page of the mysterious
FBI memorandum on something
revealed by the convicted spy
Rudolph Abel, which moved the
Bureau to reopen the case of Saville

Sax. As is so often the case with
released FBI files, this one is so
heavily redacted that we are left
with only a few enticing hints about
what happened.

eccentricity was far greater than at any other time during the twentieth century, either before or afterwards. While some people did find Savy seedy and disreputable, others regarded him as a fascinating eccentric. Sure, he lived in a fantasy world, but like, say, Michael Jackson, he had a remarkable ability to engage others in his daydreams.

Theodore Hall and Saville Sax were never charged with espionage, and we are not likely to know the full reason why until the FBI releases uncensored copies of the rest of their files. No doubt part of the reason was that the FBI feared being forced to reveal classified information, which might alert both the Soviet government and the American public to their clandestine activities. It could also be that Hall or Sax may have given information to the FBI in exchange for immunity from prosecution. Perhaps, for instance, some other agent, such as the mysterious figure code-named ADEN, made some deal with the FBI that exempted Hall from prosecution. Finally, the restraint shown may also have something to do with internal politics within the FBI.

We must remember that the culture of secrecy in the FBI enables it to pursue private agendas, which may not have much to do with either justice or the national interest. Perhaps the FBI agents, already prosecuting the Rosenbergs when they interrogated Ted and Savy, did not want to learn anything that could complicate the case in progress. On the other hand, I, myself, may here be starting to indulge in the paranoid sort of conspiracy theory that secret agencies always seem to inspire. We often think of agents such as those of the FBI as pursuing secret agendas with diabolical cleverness. For the most part, the behavior of the FBI in this case shows, so far as I can tell, little or no indication of a conspiracy but, rather, simple stupidity.

I wrote to Athan Theoharis, an expert on the FBI, in 1997 to ask about the agenda of the Bureau, and he promptly replied that, ". . . the FBI was not as competent as the public (and perhaps you) thinks . . . FBI officials were better at the 'politics of counterintelligence' than the 'practice of counterintelligence,' and their major successes were the product more of luck than skill."

It is very fortunate for me that my father was never charged with espionage, for I might never have recovered from the trauma of having a parent (perhaps both) jailed. I am far less certain that this was lucky for my father. Had the truth come out, he might have found peace of a sort that was to elude him for the rest of his life, whether he chose to cooperate with authorities or not. Perhaps he could even have used a public trial as a forum for discussion of the political context in which the espionage took place. It is also possible that he might have relished the role of martyr.

*I grew up in a world of doubles. My generation of children
had no television—ours was the age of comic books,
and in these, a superhero was nobody unless he had an
alter ego who really was nobody. Superman was really
the bespectacled Clark Kent, Captain Marvel was really
the crippled newsboy Billy Batson, Batman was really a
Scarlet Pimpernel sort of fellow who acted a playboy in
"real life" or was it the other way around?*

   —MARGARET ATWOOD,
    NEGOTIATING WITH THE DEAD

IX. Home and School

After the FBI had interviewed my father, the agents ceased making themselves conspicuous and never spoke directly to him again. My parents, nonetheless, continued to suspect that they were still being observed. They worried whenever I appeared on leftist mailing lists, and asked me not to do anything that might get my name into the newspapers. They could not explain why except in very vague terms, and their cautions sounded paranoid, even bizarre, to me. The ways they concealed their leftist views struck me as cowardly.

Because we couldn't speak of the bomb in our household, we were in actuality unable to talk about much else, at least not anything important, very well. We couldn't speak much of the way my brother still sucked his thumb and carried around a blanket at the age of six, which was considered merely a charming eccentricity. We could not meaningfully discuss my sister's cutting classes, and her wandering the streets of Chicago in search of adventure. We could not speak of the danger I faced going to school each day, as the most convenient target of kids who were angry against Whites. Nobody remarked on the way I was slipping into a perpetual daze, constantly forgetting things as I daydreamed my afternoons away. Any intense discussion of these problems in our family would almost ineluctably, sooner or later have led to the subject of the atomic bomb. This had the effect of limiting our intimacy with one another, while at the same time sealing us off from the rest of society.

Nevertheless, in many ways our family was a bit like the "typical American family" of situation comedies such as "Father Knows Best," in which the father was prone to crazy enthusiasms that the mother had to keep in check. My father and mother later in their marriage used to get into fights, for example, over makeup. She wanted to wear lipstick, while he believed that makeup was an expression of bourgeois decadence. Once when they got into a particularly vehement argument about this, my father said, "All right, I'll show you how embarrassing it is to go out with a person who wears lipstick." With that, he grabbed my mother's red lipstick and smeared it heavily across his mouth. They then went out together, as they had been planning to, the cosmetic still spread over my father's lips, and each waited to see whether the other would give up first. About a block from our home, my father ducked around a corner, pulled out a handkerchief, and wiped all the lipstick off.

Resentment between Jews and Poles or Ukrainians (the family scarcely distinguished between the two), was part of the tribal heritage of Central Europe. My father would sometimes turn livid at the mere mention of Ukrainians, but I thought that my relatives, through their continuing support for Stalin, had thereby forfeited any moral authority when it came to politics.

Chicago was very sharply divided into neighborhoods on the basis of ethnicity, class, and race. Although the physical barrier between neighborhoods often did not stretch more than a single block, one knew immediately when one had crossed into alien territory. Suddenly the houses became dramatically more opulent or squalid; signs in shop windows appeared in other languages, and people dressed differently. These various neighborhoods resembled miniature countries, ones constantly negotiating, breaking out into hostilities, or forming alliances.

For me as a child, there seemed to be three basic kinds of people in the world, in order of importance— Jews, Blacks, and everyone else. At the time, we Jews (for that is what we considered ourselves) looked upon the Blacks as our "allies," while the Poles on the far East Side were "enemies," their neighborhood a foreign and hostile country. Catholics, especially the Poles and Irish, were praying for the conversion of the Soviet Union. Distance, however, is often accompanied by wonder, and I vividly remember staring out the window of our car with fear and admiration as my parents drove through a Polish neighborhood. What caught my eye especially was a backyard altar with a small statue of the Virgin Mary, her arms outstretched, endlessly wonderful and strange.

We could talk a little about sex at home, since it was so easy to conceal the reality of that subject in rhetoric that had a nice, progressive ring. What we did not know how to discuss, however, was love; in fact, the very word sounded vaguely reactionary to us at the time. Listening to love songs became a kind of guilty pleasure. But there was also love in our family, and it managed to sustain us.

I was very romantic and yet morbidly shy, but it would never have occurred to me to ask my parents how to approach a girl. Had I asked my mother, she would probably have responded with a strained, ambiguous smile and said, with a futile sigh of sympathy, that she could give me no advice. Had I asked my father, he would probably have launched into a tirade about the evil of sexual repression. It would have been terribly abstract, and filled with Marxo-Freudian mumbo-jumbo, yet also very melodramatic. And it would have left me feeling more terrified than ever. To answer the question, my parents would have had to talk about their own experiences, and these would have been hard for them to explain without mentioning atomic espionage.

People in those days, a few decades after World War II, constantly used to talk about the "alienation" of Black kids. This was sometimes thought to be a terrible burden, though sometimes also a blessing— often, both at once. Radical leftists often looked upon American Blacks as the vanguard of a national, even a global, revolution. From my perspective, however, growing up as part of a minuscule White minority in the nearly all-Black schools of Chicago, it usually seemed that the Black kids were closer to the "mainstream" of American society than my family.

It was some time before we could afford a television. In the 1950s or early 1960s, I, along with my brother and sister, would go over to a neighbor's apartment every Thursday evening to watch "Walt Disney Presents." All week long I'd look forward to that, though probably more for the social occasion than the television show. We did eventually buy a television, a used one that was constantly breaking down. Like most kids I knew, we watched almost everything from westerns to quiz shows to sitcoms. Expressions of "mainstream" values, such as sitcoms, seemed to reach us from an enormous distance, and we watched with a combination of terror and secret longing. But perhaps the Marxism absorbed in our childhood often prepared us for them, for shows like "Leave it to Beaver," with their idealization of family life, were as utopian as any Communist tract.

"America" was something I learned about largely through textbooks and television shows. They would depict a "typical American family," in which the White suburban daddy, wearing a gray flannel suit and carrying a briefcase, kisses mommy goodbye in the morning as he got ready to commute to work. These images, of course, had nothing at all to do with life in the inner city or, I suspect, anywhere else. They were, as the leftists often said, "irrelevant." A lot of people thought that was terrible, but I thought it was great. The last thing in the world that I would have wanted to read about was the neighborhood where I went to school. "America" seemed mythical, everything I either feared or yearned for.

For a while, I took an interest in the game of chess. When Bobby Fischer, the chess champion, gave an exhibition in Chicago, playing about 50 opponents simultaneously, I even beat him. I also defeated a Latvian grandmaster. Playing first board, I led my high school team to a city championship. But I could not take the tense atmosphere of the games, so I stopped abruptly. What initially attracted me to chess, and what finally repelled me, was that it provided an insulated world, with a vocabulary, customs, and a set of values that was incomprehensible to the uninitiated. It was a bit like the circle of my grandmother or, for that matter, Communist intellectuals of the time. I yearned for acceptance and adventure in a much vaster world.

It was neither the suburbs, with all their coziness and comforts, nor the Black ghetto, with its romance, that really attracted me; rather, it was books! In elementary school I was enthralled by the folk and fairy tales of authors like Padraic Column and Andrew Lang. Later it was novels, especially those of Russians like Dostoyevski and Tolstoy. I usually had two or three close friends, and was friendly with most of the other kids in school but in a slightly distant sort of way. I was drawn to the most ancient of times as well as faraway places. When school ended, I would hurry home, open Tolstoy's *Anna Karenina*, and read until bedtime.

The African-Americans at school generally shared the American preoccupation with sports and fashion. As in most high schools at the time, differences of race and ethnicity paled in significance before the far more profound cultural difference between nerds and jocks. That distinction, however, was drawn partially on racial lines. Being Black didn't make you a jock, but being White (i.e., being "Jewish") went pretty far towards making you a nerd. As a delicate White boy, I did make a pretty easy target for "Black rage," and I was picked on, though not terribly severely. As much as anything, the Black kids regarded me with a sort of protectiveness, almost like a class pet. Once a few thugs wanted to attack me in a classroom before the teacher arrived, but the other students blocked the entrance and wouldn't let them enter.

I have wondered whether my family was unconsciously repeating an ancestral pattern. My Jewish ancestors had been persecuted and intimidated by the Ukrainian majority in their region. But their persecutors were bullied as well, by a yet more numerous and powerful ethnic group, the Russians, with whom the Jews tried to form an alliance. Now we were among Blacks instead of Ukrainians, and were linked with the predominantly White society of America rather than with ethnic Russians. Nevertheless, the archetypal model in the two situations is eerily similar.

Religion, or rather our lack of it, was another factor that set us dramatically apart from the Black majority. The Black kids were overwhelmingly Baptist. In my family, we prided ourselves on being atheists, above the prejudices of the unenlightened, and in those days atheists were full of evangelical fervor. We, the children, could not help occasionally boasting that "We don't believe in God."

One young African-American once asked me, "Do you believe in the Devil, then?"

"No," I replied.

"Shi-i-i-i-i-t," responded the young man. "He don' believe in God, and he don' believe in the Devil. I don' know where he's goin'. "

By about the fifth or sixth grade, I had learned not to be quite so open. In eighth grade, our teacher was Mrs. Rice, an African-American woman of little education, but who did have a great sense of humor and a lot of common sense, at least in most situations. She talked about the kids who were hell-raisers in the school.

One girl chimed in, "I wonder what they think of when they are in church on Sunday."

"Some of them don't even go to church on Sunday!" responded Mrs. Rice and she glared about the room, which was filled with nervous laughter.

Instruction in elementary school was of almost unrelieved monotony. A teacher might walk into the classroom and write the page number of our textbook on the board. We would then open our books and spend forty-five minutes fidgeting, but the teacher seldom even noticed that we hardly ever turned in our work. For about a year, my parents managed to enroll me in an experimental school. Like many such institutions of the early 1960s, it had reformist ideals, a bohemian ambiance, and few bureaucratic controls. The teachers were generally graduate students, who were miserably paid but permitted to do, more or less, whatever they pleased.

Once I started walking part of the way home with one of my teachers, a gentleman from the Caribbean. Though he usually seemed relaxed, witty, and charming, his favorite subject was the "sick society." Instead of worrying so much about individual neuroses, he explained, psychologists should be studying the sick society instead. One day he stopped suddenly in the middle of the sidewalk and remarked without irony, "If you are going to walk home with me you ought to learn French. At times I get so disgusted with the sick society that I am completely unable to speak its language. If that were to happen while we were walking home, I would need you to translate." As we continued on our way, I constantly wondered what I would do were he were to suddenly choke in mid-sentence, and then speak only French.

In many respects, it was my mother who, in her own humble way, did live the American dream. While working full-time, she attended Chicago Teacher's College in the evenings, where she received her B.A. and, eventually, her M.A. in library science. Among my fondest childhood memories are the times when she would talk about her classes in the evening, about Cervantes and Shakespeare. Once she even gave me one of her papers to read about the character of Caliban in Shakespeare's *The Tempest*.

In many ways, she was like the many single mothers of more recent times. While my father worked only sporadically, it was she who generally supported the family, both emotionally and financially. Bluma felt that, as the clan matriarch, she was entitled to give orders to Susan. It was right, Bluma thought, that Susan should both work and take care of the family if Savy had more important things on his mind. My father seemed not to fully belong to the family, even though he usually set the tone for it. My mother was the one who would buy the presents for Christmas/Chanukah and say that they were from both parents, although we kids knew full well that they were really only from her. Divorce was widely considered either socially unacceptable or romantically bohemian, but, if Susan ever considered that as an option, she probably never told a soul.

As my father became increasingly erratic, my mother began to look to me for a while as the proverbial "man of the house." She would sometimes talk to me about her difficulties, but I could offer little understanding and no good advice. Besides, no pre-adolescent wants to be a "mamma's boy," and I could only disappoint her. Now and then, perhaps, I knew how to sound almost like an adult, but that was just an act. One thing is worse than being a frightened, confused little kid—when you are not allowed to be one!

I have been told that the Russians paid my father for his services, but, considering the way that the family was then living, it surely couldn't have been much. My father lost his mimeographing business when he was evicted for failing to pay the rent. He had also been barred from attending classes at Roosevelt College for defaulting on his tuition. What enabled my parents to survive were checks that came regularly from Bluma. Savy probably felt uncomfortable about receiving that money, for he would often lose the checks or forget to cash them.

That may have been just as well. As the Russians probably warned my father, the FBI was reviewing his bank account to look for unexplained sums of money. In addition, they snooped into my grandmother's account to ascertain whether the checks she wrote out to her son appeared exorbitant. The Soviet agents, in any case, did not have limitless sums at their disposal, and they distrusted spies who worked for money rather than out of ideology.

My mother eventually obtained a job in the library of the University of Chicago Laboratory School. My father, meanwhile, after completing his degree in elementary education from Roosevelt College, enrolled in the Human Development program at the University of Chicago. He did well in his courses, but had great trouble completing his Masters' thesis. He had a grand theory of the cyclical nature of human emotions, which he hoped would revolutionize psychology, but his committee members could not understand a bit of it. With every request for clarification, he would respond by making the paper more complicated and obscure. After a professor criticized his figures, he returned a few weeks later to announce that he had developed an entirely new system of statistics. After Savy had been working intermittently on the thesis for about seven years, the University granted him the degree simply to be rid of him, but would not allow him to return for further study. Savy said that the committee members were not sure whether his thesis was "the prophecy of a genius or the ravings of an idiot."

I remember vividly how we often did not have dessert as children. When my mother was able to buy a pint of ice cream, she would ceremoniously cut it into five equal slices, while the rest of us would look on in silence, secretly wondering who would get the most. Later, when the family had gradually grown more affluent, my mother began to buy ice cream by the gallon. Her ritual of dividing it up then vanished completely; only our appetites remained. Everybody would scoop up the ice cream in huge spoonfuls, as much as he or she could eat, and more. Susan started to grow fat; so did the rest of us.

Eventually, with a little help from Bluma, my parents even bought a nice house. Nevertheless, we did not really know how to enjoy the amenities of middle-class life in America. We thought ourselves too good for it, or else maybe not good enough. Our middle-class status seemed strange, inappropriate, and terribly precarious, like a masquerade that was bound, sooner or later, to be exposed. But visitors from the suburbs seemed to regard my family with awe—"beatniks, genuine beatniks."

Entering adolescence in the mid-1960s, I began to see how there might be pleasure as well as fear in a "conspiratorial" sort of fellowship, when my parents would invite their friends over for drinks and late evening conversation. Many of these guests were aging refugees from the collapse of the Communist movement. For all of my life, I have been looking in vain for another such fascinating group of conversationalists. They were all people of wide reading and broad experience.

After being painfully disillusioned with political activism, most had settled into modest, relatively undemanding jobs. Some aspired to be writers, but most simply poured their considerable creative energies into talk. They were, in various degrees, alcoholics, and all had very attractive airs of pathos. They rejected the society that had seemingly discarded them, but that had the effect of creating a wonderful feeling of togetherness when they got together over drinks.

It was terribly flattering that they not only listened to me as well but even let me share the beer. As the talk continued way past my usual bedtime, it often turned to politics. Now and again, somebody would deliver a magnificently impassioned tirade about how our whole neighborhood was actually run by the Mafia, or how racist maps made Greenland look as big as Africa. But all that came to an abrupt end one evening when a close friend of my parents, grown so drunk that she could barely stand, made a preposterously awkward attempt to seduce me. "Don't you see? He was hot," she later said. "It hurts to be hot."

When I entered high school in the mid-1960s, the Civil Rights Movement was very strong in Chicago. There were constant rallies in Chicago for integration and against cuts in welfare. I doubt whether many students in grammar school or even high school really understood the issues, but demonstrations were an important part of my social life.

It was fashionable, almost a rite of passage, for young people to be arrested at demonstrations, but the arrests in those days were generally very civilized affairs. People would be held perhaps for a couple of hours, which might be filled by camaraderie and lively conversation in the jail. At one time, my mother told me that, if I wanted to get arrested, the best time was while I was still in high school. If I waited until the age of eighteen, that would give me a permanent police record.

One day there was to be a big demonstration against segregation in the Chicago schools. As I left that morning, my parents told me, quite unexpectedly, that I should not on any account end up in jail. My father, they explained, was in line for a new job, and any mention of my name in the newspapers might ruin his chances. I told my parents, truthfully, that the leaders of the march had assured us that the demonstrators would do nothing to provoke arrests.

The march took place on a hot July day. As expected, I ran into quite a few friends from school and the neighborhood, and we all marched together for a while. Then the procession stopped abruptly. We asked the marshals why, but they seemed to have no notion whatsoever. I fidgeted nervously for what certainly seemed an interminable amount of time. At first it was nice simply to be with friends, but after a while we could no longer find either ideas or energy for conversation. Finally, the marshals told us to sit down in the street. When asked, "Why?," the marshals replied, "That's the order," quickly adding that they had no intention of blocking traffic or provoking arrests.

The prospect of sitting was most welcome, and nobody felt like complaining. I was soon half asleep from the heat, when, all of a sudden I looked up. Just a few yards ahead, police were hauling demonstrators into wagons. Remembering the injunction of my parents, I got up and ran away. "What are you doing?" a girl shouted at me as I fled.

A moment later, I overheard a young mother say indignantly of the marchers, "Well, I certainly hope they had their parents' permission to get arrested." Apparently Dick Gregory, who led the march, had decided then and there to have a sit-in after all, because he was caught up in a dispute with city authorities about the procession route.

When I got home and told my parents what had happened, my father was sheepishly apologetic about having told me not to get arrested, but it was very hard to explain my behavior to friends in school. The next day at school I overhead a girl whom I was secretly interested in, also one of the small minority of White students, say that she had "never felt such brotherhood as in that jail." Only much, much later did I realize exactly why my father didn't want my name to appear in any newspaper—the FBI was still on his trail. Most leftists and cultural revolutionaries were as deeply integrated into American society as everybody else. They might adapt a pose of fashionable alienation, but they kept a very careful eye on cultural, and even economic,

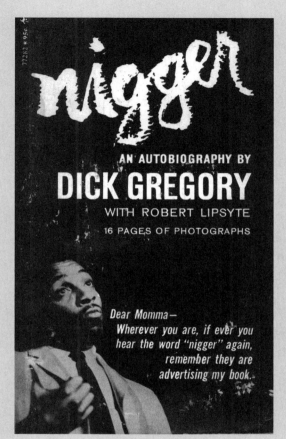

RICHARD CLAXTON "DICK" GREGORY (1932–PRESENT)

Dick Gregory was continuously organizing protests in Chicago throughout the 1960s, at first for Civil Rights and later also against the war in Vietnam. Gregory had a huge ego and always craved the spotlight.

Dick Gregory first came to public attention as a comedian, and, by placing his portrait on the dollar bill, he intended to satirize American racism. Simultaneously, he poked fun a bit at his own vanity.

trends. Our family, by contrast, felt permanently excluded, though only our parents knew why.

In the latter half of the 1960s, the Civil Rights Movement became increasingly militant. There were riots, and a new "Black Power" movement emerged whose leaders talked of armed overthrow of the government. They often quoted the dictum of Mao Tze Tung that, "Power comes from the barrel of a gun." The theatrical Stokely Carmichael, constantly photographed with a clenched fist raised above his head, incited people to insurrection. By the end of the decade the Civil Rights Movement and its rhetoric were also being exploited by violent street gangs in Chicago such as the Blackstone Rangers as a front for criminal activities including extortion, selling illegal drugs, and prostitution.

George Romney, the governor of Michigan and a leading Presidential candidate in 1968, once called for Stokely Carmichael to be tried for treason. My father, who had by that time entirely withdrawn from politics, looked at me quizzically and asked, "What do you think? Should he be tried?" Though Carmichael didn't seem much different from the gang leaders who had harassed me at school, I had only a vague idea of what treason was. But, as I later realized, my father was not really thinking about Carmichael at all.

Moorland-Spingarn Research Center, Howard University Archives, Washington, DC

STOKELY CARMICHAEL / KWAME TURE (1941–1998)

In only half a decade, Stokely Carmichael completed his meteoric rise to national stardom, radically changed his politics, and then began to slip back into obscurity. He had commenced his career as an activist by registering Black voters in Alabama, and by 1966 became Chairman of the Student Non-Violent Coordinating Committee, (SNCC), a Civil Rights organization originally closely allied with Martin Luther King, Jr.'s Southern Leadership Conference. Under his direction, this group moved from promoting racial integration to a philosophy of "Black Power" and violent confrontation. He quickly became a national celebrity, angered the collective leadership of SNCC, and soon after resigned to take a position as "Honorary Prime Minister" in the new Black Panther Party. In 1969, he rejected the party's Black Nationalism for a more extreme philosphy of racial separatism, relocated to Guinea, and changed his name to Kwame Ture. While some public leaders in both America and Africa continued to honor him as an elder statesman of Black liberation, his influence in the United States was over.

He (Zeus) moved flashing his fires incessantly,
*   and the thunderbolts,*
the crashing of them and the blaze
*   together came flying, one after*
another, from his ponderous hand,
*   and spinning whirls of inhuman*
flame, and with it the earth,
*   the giver of life, cried out*
aloud as she burned, and the vast forests
*   in the fire screamed.*

—HESIOD, *THEOGONY*
(TRANSLATION, RICHMOND LATTIMORE)

X. A Game for Children

For spies, dishonesty, together with self-deception, becomes not merely a tactic but a way of life. Espionage gives a person a second identity, turning the old one, and everything belonging to it, into a charade. Since a spy must always conceal so much of his true character, he can never really open up about anything at all. An element of dishonesty enters his relations with colleagues and other acquaintances outside his network of fellow spies. All friendship, even with those who share his engagement in espionage, is clouded, since almost anybody might be a potential informer. There is sometimes an intimacy among those engaged in espionage that is very intense, but it is very precarious as well. The big deceptions invariably entail all sorts of little ones, for both emotional and pragmatic reasons. On finally learning of my father's espionage, I felt that I had never really known him at all.

I now realize that Savy's elaborately abstract mode of thinking was a way of filtering experience to protect his fantasy world, thus keeping at a distance a society he neither trusted nor understood. Once when my sister had run away from home, Savy tried to persuade her to return by talking about zoology. Starting with the amoeba and going on to the elephant and chimpanzee, he argued that those animals that are "higher" on the evolutionary scale spend increasingly longer periods with their parents. Savy used to discourse on Freud's theory of the primal father, who monopolized all of the women, and he seemed to relish that role a bit too much.

Savy was prone to sophistry, in large part because of his lack of social graces. Elaborate reasoning was a substitute for intuition, for the ability to read all sorts of social signs and signals. Their atomic espionage meant that both Ted and Savy would never be able to talk openly about the most significant experiences of their lives. Caution and reticence were habits that became impossible to break. Espionage, were its consequences not so serious, would be the sort of game that would interest children. There is a juvenile "naughtiness" about it; it is, one could say, "mischief" on an international scale. It combines an extreme idealism, even a sort of "innocence," with a terrifying capacity to hurt. The most familiar expressions of this are adolescent fantasies about James Bond and the like.

I know well how betrayal in a friendship or marriage, or even a small circle of friends, often hurts people so profoundly that they are moved to doubt both the goodness of men and the justice of God. The most brilliant rationalizations for atomic espionage sound trivial if we imagine a nuclear bomb falling on a major city like New York or Washington, DC. However idealistic their motives may possibly have been at times, this was the prospect that the atomic spies were willing to accept. It was not simply a symbolic attack on some abstract entity known as "America." It was death for family, friends, and colleagues, along with millions of others. This ought, it seems to me, to have easily overruled any arguments for atomic espionage based on vague theories and speculative calculations. As one of the millions who might have been killed, it is hard for me not to take atomic espionage personally.

But even if we were to accept the passing of plans for the atomic bomb to the Russians as a defensive measure, intended to give the Soviet Union a basic security through "mutually assured destruction" or "MAD," this does not apply to the passing of further secrets by Hall and possibly my father. Throughout his life, Hall continued to deny that he had passed secrets of the hydrogen bomb, and Joan Hall reaffirmed this to me after he had died. These denials, however, do not seem at all credible, and they also place the veracity of the couple in question.

In his memoirs, KGB officer Vladimir Chikov stated that Theodore Hall (that is, the agent with the code name MLAD, meaning "young") had recruited two physicists, code-named ANTA and ADEN, who passed information to the Soviet Union about the hydrogen bomb. Their courier, according to Chikov, had the code-name CTAR or "OLD," which was later revealed to be the pseudonym that had been used to refer to my father.[38] Chikov's memoirs are generally considered to be reliable in their broad outline but not so in specific details. He sometimes may have deliberately included misinformation to protect his sources or to satisfy the Russian censors. The clandestine archive kept by KGB agent Vassily Mitrokhin, however, confirmed that Ted Hall returned to espionage in 1948 and recruited two agents, one of whom had the code name ADEN, to pass information on the hydrogen bomb to the Soviet Union.[39] My mother later told me that Hall had recruited a physicist to engage in espionage, one who would eventually commit suicide and leave behind his wife and children. Joseph Albright and Marcia Kunstel also confirm in *Bombshell* that both Ted and Savy returned to espionage in 1948, though they do not specify whether the secrets they helped to pass included information on the hydrogen bomb. The authors argue that what Hall passed to the Soviet Union probably included the plans for a secret isotope-producing process to be used in the mass production of nuclear weapons.[40] Perhaps, as so often happens with spies, the activity of espionage continued largely on its own momentum after the ideals that inspired it have been largely forgotten.

Still, the stealing of the plans to construct an atomic bomb and related acts of espionage were conducted by relatively young men, perhaps in a state of emotional intoxication. They perceived their acts as holy transgressions, like the creation of the atomic bomb itself. But they may have been less exceptional than either they or their critics wanted to believe.

For David Greenglass, the spy who implicated the Rosenbergs, the cause of Communism had faded into near insignificance, and his final loyalty was not to any universal ideal but to his immediate family. He had already lost interest in the Socialist movement and cooperated with the United States government, not for entirely selfish reasons—for he probably did not receive a reduced sentence in return—but to obtain exemption of his wife from prosecution. At the opposite pole is Julius Rosenberg, who sacrificed not only the truth but himself and his wife as well in the pursuit of the Socialistic ideals. My grandmother, Bluma Sax, was motivated primarily by Russian nationalism, though it was given an ideological veneer. My father, Saville Sax, was motivated by something even grander than Communism, a belief in the nearly unlimited powers of humankind.

The most elusive motivations were Ted Hall's, who has left us an implausible description of his espionage being the result of complicated technocratic calculations. No doubt part of his motivation was hubris, the notion that he could manipulate the course of history. Hall could act conceited as a young man, as my mother discovered when she visited him and his wife the day after Christmas in the early 1950s. They were making fun of all their presents and of the people who had given them. That, however, was perhaps not much more than a bit of extended adolescence, and Ted did not appear arrogant in his later years.

Once, toward the late 1960s, Ted returned briefly from England and visited Savy in Chicago. By that time the two old friends had almost nothing left in common. Ted had become a Cambridge don, completing a transformation that began when he and his brother changed the family name from Holtzberg to Hall. He had picked up many of the ways of the British upper middle class. Savy, disheveled as ever, had a decidedly plebian manner; in fact, he came across as somewhat of a huckster. The two of them sat together fidgeting nervously for about an hour, when Hall, his social obligation having been fulfilled, got up and left.

*. . . .destroyed by madness, starving hysterical
naked, dragging themselves through the negro
streets at dawn looking for an angry fix. . . .*

—ALLEN GINSBERG, *HOWL*

XI. The Nineteen Sixties and After

The era of the Cold War began to draw to an end in the period we
know as the "Sixties" (about 1967–1972), when just about everyone I knew went crazy. They all felt the seductive call of the "street,"
a world in which absolutely anything could happen. This was the
society that would hang out in all-night restaurants and on street cor-
ners, exchanging gossip, and waiting for adventures. It was filled with
artists, hippies, con men, addicts, Communists, Ayn-Randians, and
gangsters. Stories about mayhem and magic were everywhere. The
young stranger who sat down next to you might suddenly announce
that he was the reincarnated Joan of Arc. Legends abounded about
karate champions who could catch bullets in mid-air, and robbers
who literally hypnotized the police. There were also men and women
who claimed not to have, or believe in, names. One explained, "When

I had a name, people would think of my name and not of me, so I got rid of it!"

The person whom I found most impressive was Pete, who I now would call a "young man," though he seemed very old to me at the time. Pete had completed college without ever once getting a grade less than "A." On graduation, he had taken a job as a janitor, and devoted most of his time to working on a metaphysical system, which soon rivaled Hegel's in complexity. The foundation was the destruction of knowledge. In Pete's words, "Everything is true, because the truth is everything. Whatever is is. Therefore, everything is true." He made these pronouncements with such serenity that the local gangsters were intimidated.

There were many self-proclaimed prophets in the street, among the most successful of whom was a middle-aged man going by the name of "Om." He claimed to be "all knowledge, all power, and all perfection, beyond God and beyond the beyond of God." Since Om believed that money was the source of all evils in the world, he decided to go into business, and planned to be so successful that he would literally make "all the money in the world." Then, he intended to "abolish money." In 1973 Om and his followers would be arrested for counterfeiting money.[41]

There was one tough guy in particular who knew how to titillate, frighten and fascinate almost everybody he encountered. He seemed to be "king of the street," and was constantly drawing an audience with his stories about gangs and Mafiosi. My mother would run into him again decades later, when she worked at a homeless shelter in Tucson, and he wandered in for a meal and a bed. By then he was toothless, bloated, and old before his time.

The Sixties are often remembered as a time of "youth rebellion," but that is not accurate. The leaders of the so-called "youth-culture" were all either, like Frank Zappa and Jerry Rubin, entering middle age, or else, like Timothy Leary and Allen Ginsberg, already old. Except in covert ways, the generation of my parents had been deprived of opportunities for adolescent rebellion, in fact they were often called the "silent generation of the 1950s." Many adults of that era had been denied a normal adolescence by either World War II or the Korean War, in which they were forced to submit themselves to a military kind of discipline. Later, they had been intimidated by McCarthyism. What made the late 1960s so turbulent was that these two generations went through an adolescent rebellion at the same time. For the generation of my parents it was a belated one, far too late, but for my generation it came much too early. The culture-wars of the 1960s and 1970s were much like conventional wars such as Vietnam, where older people on both sides pushed the young to risks that they themselves would not take, thus enjoying vicarious glory and excitement. Savy, seeing the turbulence of the Sixties as his long-awaited revolution, became something of a hippy.

One day before a big test at school, I spoke to Savy in irritation. As I was leaving the house Savy ran after me and tackled me. He pinned me to the ground and hit me, then got up, turned, and lumbered back inside. I cried for the entire day, looking like a wimp in a dangerous neighborhood and doing very badly on my exam. A few days later, my mother told me, in an almost casual way, that she wondered whether the attack on me showed that my father was "insane."

Not terribly long after that, my father talked about how he played "Russian roulette" while driving on the highway, closing his eyes for a short while and then opening them to see if he was still alive. "Destroyer! Destroyer! Arenberg is the king of the Destroyers," he shouted at my mother, ". . . and you are the queen!"

One evening, as I was studying, my mother suddenly approached me and said, "I've arranged to have Savy taken away to a mental hospital. The men will be arriving soon. I just thought you ought to know." Without giving me time to reply, she hurried into the next room and shut the door. I left my home in panic and confusion, walked around the block and tried to gather my thoughts.

Then I returned and looked at the house from a distance as a van was pulling up. Some indistinct figures got out, went to the door, and then, after a while, returned to the vehicle and pulled away. I continued to watch for what may have been only about five minutes but seemed like hours, before returning home. When I walked into the

United States Senate Historical Office, Washington

SENATOR JOSEPH RAYMOND "JOE" MCCARTHY (1908–1957)

For many today, the word "McCarthyism" is practically synonymous with paranoia. Senator Joe McCarthy made little distinction between Communists and other leftists, the so-called "fellow-travellers." He thought that both were out to destroy the United States. McCarthy presumed that anyone with even a vague association with a Communist must also be one, especially if that person hesitated to deny his/her affiliation, even under cover of the Fifth Amendment. Fueled by hefty consumption of alcohol, his charges became increasingly wild, until he alleged that the American Army was heavily infiltrated by Communists, prompting the Senate to censor him in 1954.

Seated at the table in the forefront is Joseph Welch, chief counsel for the United States Army, holding one of his hands to his head in apparent disbelief at what the Senator was saying. In this highly televised encounter, Welch uttered his now famous statement of contempt, "Have you no sense of decency?"

living room, I found my mother and father sitting sullenly together. The experience of spying had served my father well, and he knew exactly how to handle such a crisis. He had challenged the papers of the mental hospital, and it turned out that they did not grant them authority to have him taken away. Then my father triumphantly suggested to the visitors that they should really take his wife to the funny farm instead.

Shortly afterwards, my father moved out of our home to set up housekeeping with a mistress, who promptly dumped him. He then wandered about aimlessly and talked of suicide, until he suddenly received a job as Program Director of a new-age project in Education at the University of Southern Illinois in Edwardsville. There, Savy finally had an opportunity to live out the fantasies of a lifetime.

The man who had lived a life of secrecy now proclaimed a cult of total openness. Following his example, people talked endlessly about their sex lives. All of a sudden, Savy became a veritable Henry Kissinger, with a crowd of middle-aged women practically fighting over him. One in particular used to listen intently as Savy discoursed on the theory of progressive pedagogy. Then she would smile, roll her eyes and say, "That's a good example of SAXology." After a number of casual affairs, my father eventually settled on a steady girlfriend, seemingly the sort of "nice Jewish girl" his parents might have wanted for him. After living together with him for a couple of years, however, she decided to become a lesbian.

All three of us kids in my family started to hang out with hustlers and low-lifes. My mother found it very hard to object to the company we kept, after having in her earlier years been called "criminal" and worse for her militant support of racial integration. Besides, she had a special affection for "lost souls."

My sister Sarah had been an awkward teenager, but when, at the age of 13 or 14, she began to cut classes and join the counterculture, people suddenly looked on her almost as a goddess. Savy once told me that she had several "Zen-Buddhist experiences." When I did not appear properly impressed, he slyly accused me of being "jealous."

My brother Joshua had been the best student as well as the best athlete in the family. Furthermore, he seemed to be the most "normal" of us all. Such "mundane" accomplishments, however, brought him far less recognition than Sarah received for her flamboyance or I had for my dreamy aloofness.

I much later found a letter from Susan's mother, Winifred Healy, dated November 18, 1968, that describes her grandchildren, starting with me:

> *He is a brilliant kid but is having the uncomfortable experience of alienation that so many young kids have. I suppose Susan's divorce hasn't helped but he seems to be fond of both his parents—maybe that's part of the trouble, but I really think it's much more than that; it's this general malaise that is flooding the world. Boria, my grandson, came to visit me late in the summer, and he stayed a week with me, and we had a wonderful visit. We had no trouble with communication, but that is what he complains of in his family. I suspect it is partly his fault, and that he doesn't try enough himself to communicate. He has an apartment of his own now in Chicago, which is sad, but I guess he'll just have to go through this thing till he gets it out of his system.*
>
> *Sarah, the middle child, is now 17 and very attractive and talented and interesting. But—I shudder to say it—she is one of America's hippies. She disappeared last May. At that time, Susan and her husband (Saville then) were tipped off that Sarah had gone to New York, so they went there and found her and brought her back. Saville is now teaching at the University of Southern Illinois at Edwardsville, and he took back Sarah with him. In a few weeks she disappeared again, and this time they were not able to locate her, and she remained away several months. Finally, just a few weeks ago, she suddenly came back, having been to Canada, the Grand Canyon, and God knows where else. But, as soon as her father found out that she was at home, he came to Chicago to get her, and she disappeared*

again, and is still away. No-one knows where. Don't ask me how she does it—I don't know. I only know I love her, and believe in an awful lot of good in her. . . .

The youngest son, Josh, is fifteen, and six feet tall. He came for a visit with me too last spring. He is the most stable and steady of the lot, and very intelligent too. He seems to have a good relationship with Susan's new husband, and Jeff is wonderful with him. So, at least we have that to comfort us. . . .

But, though almost nobody realized it at the time, Josh was the most psychologically vulnerable of us all, for his feelings were far from the surface. When Savy beat my brother once too often, the young man picked up a brick and threatened to break open his father's skull.

During a visit to Savy in Edwardsville, Joshua turned an axe on himself and deliberately cut off a toe, and then chatted amiably to people as they searched for the lost appendage. Savy tried to hold my brother a virtual prisoner in his house, threatening to have him "institutionalized" if he made any attempt to leave. My father was trying to be the therapist for his own family, and had developed an elaborate theory about Joshua's mental illness and how to cure it.

A couple of months later, I helped my brother escape in the middle of the night, and we hitchhiked to upstate New York. Joshua and I lived together for a few months, supporting ourselves on welfare and odd jobs, but my brother soon lost his mind completely and ended up in a mental hospital. Once when I visited him, the guards got the two of us mixed up, thought I was my brother trying to escape, and hauled me back to the ward. That entire period was probably the lowest point of my life, and it is impossible for me to look back on it without a shudder. Fortunately, I was too caught up in the great adventure of growing up to realize how desperate my situation had become, and that ignorance protected me from despair.

I found a temporary job as a counselor in a summer camp and moved to another town. Then Joshua escaped from the hospital, and hitchhiked back to Savy in Edwardsville. For the next several years, my brother drifted from place to place, constantly in and out of mental institutions and jails. Without the use of drugs, he would hallucinate. Once an inner voice told him to jump out of a third-story window; he obeyed, almost killing himself.

My sister wound up in a mental hospital as well, but soon escaped. She too then went to live with her father, who, in a fit of possessiveness, laid an elaborate series of curfews on her. When she failed to keep them, Savy threatened to fast "until death." When caught with his fingers in a cake, he said, "I'm not eating, only tasting." A bit older than my sister and brother, I was perhaps a trifle less vulnerable. I tried to rebel by being "conservative" as much as I dared (which wasn't much).

After a few years, Savy's following began to disperse. Though still occasionally able to fascinate people with his kooky brilliance, Savy, entering his mid-fifties, could no longer convincingly play the role of a precocious adolescent. He boasted to everybody about his atomic espionage, despite the fact that Ted Hall was still alive. As he related the story, however, Hall had become, in any case, a very peripheral figure who barely merited a passing mention. Savy had conceived and executed the entire plot, with Hall merely following his lead.

Perhaps Savy was bothered by the contradiction between his New Age creed of absolute honesty and his own former life of utter secrecy. It may also be that he was sensing the approach of death and felt an urge to confess, a desire to make his peace with the world. It is also entirely possible that he began to speak about his espionage partly out of anger towards Ted Hall, who had shared his adventure, stolen his girlfriend, and left him to take the consequences. Had word of Savy's boasting gotten back to the FBI, it could have placed the Halls in jeopardy.

But even as he was boasting about his dangerous exploits, he wrote in a notebook I later found, "Just consider where the threat of being destroyed by atomic warfare is greatest— in countries with huge stock-piles of bombs like the United States and Russia, or in countries with no atomic weapons at all like Nicaragua or Chile? Everyone that I have asked sees the United States and Russia as much less safe than countries lacking in atomic hardware." The passage is a good example of the fragmentary insights he would often make but could never follow up. It suggests that he may have been more troubled about his espionage than he ever showed.

Amazingly, the FBI agents who were following Savy failed to note either the chaos of his personal life or his boasting about espionage. The FBI closed its last file on my father in 1969, but his sense of danger and suspicion haunted him until the end of his life.

Contrary to what people sometimes thought, my father was far from being a "free spirit." Most of what he did or said was elaborately, if often inaccurately, calculated for effect. He may have projected the trendy alienation of a beatnik or an intellectual of the 1950s. For such people, that pose generally masked an indirect accommodation with the society they pretended to despise. But for him, the image concealed a far deeper alienation. This estrangement had begun when his parents, immigrants from a distant countryside, first confronted the disorienting tumult of New York City. It developed into the isolation of the expatriate, the traitor, trying to make his way in a country to which he could no longer claim a bond.

On some level, perhaps, my father had lived his life as a sort of performance before an imagined audience. It can seem flattering to have people following you around and going through your trash. In an era when many people worry that their lives might be without significance, the spy is constantly reminded how nothing in his life is trivial. The shadowy existence of a spy resembles the public one of a celebrity, yet both are often vacuous in the end.

Savy lived out his few remaining years in relative peace and obscurity. Here again, we may be reminded of the Greek Prometheus. The other important figures of Greek mythology had several stories, but he had only one. When Hercules had slain the eagle that gnawed his liver, and broken his chains, Prometheus seemed to lose all significance. He retained an honored if modest place in the Greek pantheon, yet provided no assistance to any heroes, and he made no more trouble for the other immortal beings.

We all take our experience for granted, especially as we are growing up. Like most young people, I never thought to question whether my family was anything but typical. Only by distancing myself from all that has transpired have I been able to learn lessons that could be helpful in my own life. My sister Sarah, my brother Joshua, and I continue struggling with our father's legacy. There are countless things, large and small, that middle class Americans take more or less for granted but which I had to learn laboriously. I did not have any idea how a person studies for a career, holds a job, pays his debts, and even saves money. To learn these things was a painful and arduous process, made more difficult by the way "bourgeois" values were constantly mocked in the 1960s as I came of age.

Perhaps the most difficult task for me has been to lay my father's paranoia aside. Even to criticize the institutions of America constructively, one must feel reasonably comfortable with them. One cannot operate on the assumption that the people who run government and business are in reality all secret Nazis, just waiting for an opportunity to gas the rest of us. In the squalid world of espionage, people learn to mistrust appearances, to constantly look for secret agendas. On a moderate level, this may be healthy skepticism, but for the spy or agent it is often taken to an extreme that verges on madness.

My father left me positive legacies as well as negative ones. Having learned the mores of American society relatively late in life, I am now unable to take these for granted. Like Savy, I have often been able to understand familiar scenes in unexpected ways. My residual alienation from American society has been a source of creativity as well as stress.

How could my father, or any human being for that matter, live with passing secrets used in the manufacture of the atomic bomb? How could this country live with the prospect of annihilation through atomic weapons during the Cold War? And how, for that matter, can we live with the many apocalyptic threats, from ecological collapse to terrorism, that face us today? Somehow, we do, but I suspect that we are more traumatized than we usually realize. There is a horror that accompanies us through our daily routines, surfacing from time to time but usually beyond the scope of our awareness. We may call it "the Holocaust," "terrorism," "environmental devastation," and many other things, but I suspect that on some emotional level these are all pretty much the same. My father was simply a little bit closer to this terror than most people are, and so, for that matter, am I.

When writing about him, I always feel that my words are a personal confession. I understand something about my father's mentality, since we share both genes and experiences, and I resemble him more than I really care to admit. At times I will hear his voice emerging from my mouth, or look into the mirror and see some of his features. He has always been a negative model for me, a sort of person that I didn't wish to become.

When I first learned about my father's espionage, I thought that he and his partner were rather like those Germans who gave support to the Nazi government but later denied that they knew anything about the Holocaust. I still see an analogy, but there is an important difference. I once assumed that all of those Germans had been lying, but now I am not so sure. Many really did not know much about the Holocaust, and my father surely didn't know very much about the GULAG. The judgment on both Nazis and Bolsheviks seems a little more problematic than it once did. The espionage continues to evoke a feeling of revulsion in me, but now that sense of horror has merged into the undercurrent of terror that has become a part of our daily lives.

Somehow, my father learned to live with the knowledge that he had passed atomic secrets to the Russians, and he paid a terrible price in alienation, as did all of his children. As a society, I suspect that we are, without being aware of it, also paying for our role in the development and rationalization of these weapons. Our seemingly limitless appetite for trivial entertainments shows how difficult it is to distract ourselves from a terror that never quite goes away. Perhaps the greatest irony in this story is that this man, Savy, who passed plans to build weapons to the enemies of his country was actually totally American, as much so as anyone that I have ever known and more than most.

He was American in his optimism, his ambition, his heedlessness, his proneness to sudden enthusiasms, his faith in technology, and his self-destructive impulses. I cannot think of another person who believed in the American Dream as strongly as he did.

Savy could be "almost" a lot of things—almost brilliant, almost generous, and almost wise. He seemed to be forever at the point of some epiphany that never quite arrived. In his last years, Savy at times even seemed to have achieved a sort of melancholy wisdom. Through his tantrums and his whims, he had by then managed to alienate almost everybody he knew. His family would probably have forgiven everything including physical abuse, if he had only asked. It could even be that he wanted to do so and was just waiting for the right moment. If that is so, there were two major problems. First of all, he did not have very much time. Secondly, he had not even begun to come to terms with his atomic espionage. He had alternately glorified or blocked it from his mind. In consequence, he could not make his peace with others, or the world.

The image he tried to project during his last years was that of a carefree, fun-loving, son-of-a-gun, mugging shamelessly for the camera. In a pamphlet on his New-Age therapies entitled *Wake the Dragon*, Savy wrote an autobiographical statement of about 1,000 words. Missing from his account were Bluma, the Halls, espionage, Communism, his marriage and children. Included were his jobs as a construction worker, fisherman, psychologist, and educator.[42] He could go on endlessly about things like "getting in touch with your inner self" or "being centered and rooted." He himself seemed to have no conflicts, simply because he had no past.

In early 1980, Savy collapsed from a heart attack. His doctor advised him to remain in the hospital, but he insisted on returning home. The doctor told him to at least stay in bed and avoid any exertion. Instead, on the way back, Savy bought a set of weights at a yard sale, and then stopped to go swimming. He seemed to be inviting death in other ways as well. Though his car had no brakes except for the emergency break, he refused to get the vehicle fixed. In addition, as we found out after his death, the gas tank of his car was almost rusted through. He regularly added water to the gasoline, on a theory that this would make the car drive more smoothly.

Savy died on September 25, 1980 of a heart attack while in his bathtub, and was not found for three days. My brother, by that time, had taken to calling him "the man who used to be my father." But, for all his failings, the personality of my father would not fade easily into oblivion. My sister, brother, and I all found ourselves constantly obsessing about him, often imagining him looking out from the next world. We were never quite sure whether to laugh at him, mourn him, pity him, curse him, or search our memories of his words for some fragmentary wisdom.

Whenever I hear of a young terrorist who has jeopardized the lives of others and thrown his own away, I think of my father. Then comes a rush of emotions; I am hurt and angry. At times, I am heartbroken. There is no way ever to know, but it is possible that had I as a young man been placed in a comparable position, I could also have been drawn into a sordid world like that of espionage. Perhaps a combination of idealism and alienation might have overpowered my hold on common sense.

A bit like a parent, I feel an impulse to excuse Savy's acts or, when that is impossible, to try at least to explain them. He always seemed a bit like a precocious child, with vast potential but far less in the way of accomplishment. He did have raw courage, that, had he been accepted into the military, might perhaps have made him into a hero or martyr of World War II. He was as impulsive as a child, and he had an unbounded appetite for attention. He could be very charming but was also totally unreliable.

My father could be brilliant as well as endlessly silly, gentle as well as brutal. On the eve of my wedding the family had a brief reunion at a Chinese restaurant. At the end of the meal we were brought fortune cookies, and mine read, "Reconsider any big decision." When I read it aloud, Savy smiled graciously and said, "Maybe he has reconsidered and come to the same conclusion." He was adept at working with his hands, and even showed ability as an amateur painter.

Increasingly toward the end of his life, I sensed an enormous vulnerability in Savy and wished that I, or somebody, could truly reach him. Nobody did. At times, I feel ashamed not to have tried much harder, even though it could hardly have done much good. At the time, I still thought of his having committed espionage as at most a distant possibility. It was simply one more in a host of extravagant boasts, daydreams, and theories that he proclaimed. But Savy had a way of drawing people into his fantasy world, and I needed, in order to survive, to distance myself from him.

Just for this chapter, I will leave my father with the last word. Here is a poem Savy used to conclude a privately published chapbook in the 1940s, not very long after his atomic espionage occurred:

> *Judge,*
> *See the man before you.*
> *Look deeply past the appearance*
> *Till his cone absorbs your cone.*
> *See the government*
> *Through you*
> *Through him.*
> *The sky, the sun,*
> *The streets, the avenues*
> *Through you,*
> *Through him.*
> *Look deep*
> *And see that what is you is him.*
> *Then as you condemn him*
> *You condemn yourself.*[43]

If we had a keen vision of all that is ordinary in human life, it would be like hearing the grass grow or the squirrel's heart beat, and we would die of that roar which is the other side of silence.

—GEORGE ELIOT, *MIDDLEMARCH*

Afterword

I was named after my grandfather, perhaps by my father in penance for having allegedly killed his sire. Often, I have been angry with both my father and grandfather, who traded in millennia of Jewish tradition for a vacuous set of abstractions. The Marxist ideology collapsed, leaving me with nothing. At times I have played with the idea of converting to Judaism, though never very seriously. Once a heritage has been abandoned it may be replaced, but it can never be recreated. Throughout my life I have constantly longed not only for a father but for a people.

My father had killed his father, at least so he sometimes thought. His father, in turn, must have outraged his predecessors by abandoning Judaism for Communism. When rebellion becomes a tradition, the rule of custom is especially difficult to evade. To fight against such a tradition simply binds you to it more firmly. And yet the tradition that was handed down to me is one that I cannot accept. We all, I believe, have some obligation to atone for, or at least come to terms with, the failings of our parents and ancestors. I have often thought that, say, the descendants of a Southerner who held slaves, or the children of a German who served the Nazis must have a relatively easy time of this, since they would find more public support in this than I.

Perhaps because he was afraid of provoking youthful rebellion, my father never taught me to call him "Dad." He was always "Savy," just as my mother was "Susan." This bothered me, and not only because it was different from the pattern in the households of my friends. Others may have thought calling one's parents by their first names had an appealing informality or a progressive mystique. For me, it suggested that they did not really want to be my parents. At the same time, if I had suddenly started calling them "Mom" and "Dad," it would have felt very strange and, to them at least, would have sounded stranger. They might have looked a bit startled and wondered whom I thought I was addressing.

My parents did love their children, I am sure, but they were not very good at showing love. Without quite realizing how it happened, both suddenly had found themselves married with children at a comparatively young age. They were still thinking of themselves almost as teenagers, and they were not prepared to assume the roles of "Mom" and "Dad."

For most of their 18-year marriage, my mother subordinated herself completely to my father. His dreams and career always came first. But her submission was always grudging, especially since he made poor use of the opportunities she provided. Most of the time she turned her resulting rage inward and became sullen. After the marriage ended, she became more open and maternal. While still calling her "Susan" to her face, I felt that she had finally become my mother.

Traditionally, reconciliation with one's father often comes as one enters maturity and begins to see the world as he does, perhaps even through becoming a father oneself. But this can only happen in societies that are comparatively traditional, and where the same cycles may be experienced from one generation to the next. Both my father and I longed for reconciliation, but it never came; in part, because we had not played our respective roles, even poorly. He had not learned to be a father, and I did not know how to be a son. The ultimate reason was a deed that he would never share with me nor, had he done so, I condone.

But do I love him? When I began this book, I might have answered, "no." But I am reaching a point in life where indignation begins to fall away. I now worry increasingly less about how I appear to others or ought to feel. Rightly or not, a voice rises within me to answer—"yes." I wish that I could go back in time and offer him some words of comfort or condolence. But even today, and even in fantasy, I do not know what those words would be. What might have happened if, in my family, we had talked more readily of anger, love, hurt, and even atomic bombs? I will never know, but am weary of keeping silent, and that is why I write about them now. I have rescued events of my boyhood from oblivion, and perhaps it might have been better to simply let them vanish forever, but I felt a duty to the past.

Those involved in espionage can almost never make good spouses or parents. In one passage from his memoir that I found particularly chilling, Alexander Feklisov, one of the Soviet handlers of Julius Rosenberg, wrote that agents sent to the West by Stalin always had to be married because, "In the world of espionage, a beautiful woman is one of the most tempting ways to turn an agent."[44] Feklisov was certainly lying about the reason, just as he had lied so many times before. A married agent might be seduced, just like a single one. The Soviets wanted their agents to be married so that the wife and children would remain at home as potential hostages, against whom the state might retaliate if the agent went over to the other side. For a Soviet agent, then, even marrying became an act of exploitation and at least incipient betrayal. Feklisov dutifully married, simply so he could abandon his wife for adventures in a distant land.

The atomic bomb is a disaster of such proportions that it constantly brings to mind, and even exceeds, the catastrophes described in the Bible. Christians may think of the Book of Revelations, while

ALEXANDER SEMYONOVICH FEKLISOV (1914–2007)

Feklisov, the son of a railway signalman, was always proud of his proletarian origins. After being trained in spycraft, he moved to New York in 1941, and soon began working as the handler for many prominent spies including the Rosenbergs and Klaus Fuchs. Feklisov also claimed to have had a major role in defusing the Cuban Missile Crisis of 1962, by negotiating behind the scenes. After his official retirement, he published a memoir in 2001 entitled *The Man Behind the Rosenbergs*. By that time, he had come to think of Stalin as a tyrant, lost interest in Communism, and developed an admiration for former Soviet dissident Alexander Solzhenitsyn. Nevertheless, Feklisov expressed no regrets about his espionage. He had enjoyed cloak-and-dagger intrigues as a sort of sport, and justified them as acts of Russian patriotism. In the photo above, taken in 1966, Feklisov is paying his respects at the graves of Julius and Ethel Rosenberg by sprinkling a handful of soil from his garden in Russia on their graves.

Jews need only consider the famines, plagues, and wars recorded in the accounts of ancient Israel, or perhaps Sodom and Gomorrah. And near the beginning of it all stands Abraham, the father of the Jewish faith. But I must say that, in his family at least, he was not much of a father. His first son was Ishmael, whom he had with his Egyptian slave Hagar. He allowed his wife Sarah to so mistreat Hagar that the slave ran away with her son and almost perished. Hagar did return, but, later, at his wife's urging, Abraham himself drove Hagar and Ishmael into the desert.

Abraham was hardly more fatherly to Isaac, his second son, whom he had with Sarah. When Yahweh demanded Isaac as a human sacrifice, Abraham complied. He bound his son, and was about to slit Isaac's throat when an angel appeared, pointed to a sheep, and directed Abraham to sacrifice the animal instead. The command to sacrifice had been a test, and for his willingness to honor the command Yahweh promised to bestow blessings upon Abraham and his descendants.

Abraham is honored by Jews, Christians, and Muslims, but not without much ambivalence. Rabbinical commentators have noted that Abraham was never granted a third son, and wondered whether he was ever forgiven by Isaac. Arab Muslims trace their ancestry to the wayward Ishmael, whom Abraham sent away. For Christians, the sacrifice and redemption of Isaac anticipates the crucifixion and resurrection of Jesus. According to the Gospels of both Matthew (27:47) and Mark (15:34), the final words of Jesus on the cross were "My God, my God, why have you deserted me?" But in the Gospel of Luke, the last words are "Father, into your hands I commit my spirit" (23:46, Jerusalem translation). In Christianity, God the Father will usually be overshadowed by Jesus, Mary, and even the Holy Spirit, yet a longing for him always remains. The Father in Christianity is perhaps a bit as in my family, dominant in ways yet also marginalized.

Judaism is the religion of God the Father. It has been remarkably prolific in generating new faiths, most notably Christianity, Islam, and Communism. Throughout the Jewish Bible, there are bitter, at times murderous, conflicts between fathers and sons: Noah and Ham,

Abraham and Isaac, Isaac and Jacob, Jacob and most of his sons, David and Absalom, and so on. Finally, and perhaps inevitably, Judaism itself, the religion of the father, was challenged by Christianity, the religion of the son.

In many respects, my life has followed the pattern of my father, for I also have wavered for a long time, uncertain of how to spend my life, and have done more than my share of menial jobs. Not burdened by an act such as espionage, however, I have been far steadier than he. I was able to work hard, even without knowing my calling. I tried to be all the things that he was not; if Savy had a violent temper, I was very slow to anger. If Savy acted impulsively, I learned, with difficulty, to be thorough and methodical. I have been trying to redeem my father by being the sort of person he might have, or should have, been. I have felt his fear and his anguish, and I see far too much of him in myself.

The insecurities of my childhood left me with a great yearning for moral purity. I always thought that desire was a rebellion against my father. Indeed, his behavior was in ways worse than I have recorded, for there is still a lot I will not say. But buried under all of the perverse behavior and the long-winded rationalizations, he felt the same craving for righteousness.

My own experience doing factory work makes it a bit easier for me to imagine how my father may have felt during his formative years. The stifling monotony of manual labor can be greatly reduced if one can establish a sort of rhythm. I found this out, for example, when I was employed in a scissors factory in a small upstate New York town. My assignment was called "the straps," the least desirable task in the entire factory—to quickly slip the inside handle of a scissors through a rapidly rotating belt which would grind off rough edges on the metal. Since I was not terribly skilled or agile, my hands became covered with cuts and burns, but often the rhythmic motions induced a sort of trance. Then I made far fewer mistakes and the day would pass very quickly indeed. Nearly meaningless though the work was, I also had the feeling of leaving everyday cares behind and entering a timeless realm. To work, I learned, is also to dream.

Reaching adulthood in the late 1960s and early 1970s, I did many of the same things as my contemporaries, from smoking pot to participating in student protests. I was mostly going through the motions, however, unable to share the spirit of my peers. Having grown up in a household continually near the brink of chaos, I could not readily identify with the rhetoric of "liberation." The rebellion of others was my conformity, while their conformity was often my rebellion. Where I came from, White was Black and Black was White. I lacked those experiences that everybody was supposed to have had: ecstasy on hearing rock n' roll on the radio for the first time, making out in the back of a car. . . . The rhetoric of my companions did not seem stirring, and their jokes usually didn't make me laugh. People of that era often seemed to be enraged at society, but I suspect that their anger was mostly an affectation.

It was not until I entered college that, for the first time, I found myself constantly surrounded by other White people, with only an occasional Black face. It was at first a confusing and disorienting experience. Just as I was engaged in discovering White America, White America was discovering Black culture. This was the latter 1960s, in the aftermath of the Otto Kerner Report that viewed America as moving toward two societies, "White and Black, separate and unequal." Everybody seemed to be talking in tones of the greatest earnestness and solemnity about "what life is really like in the Negro ghetto" and "what the little Black boys in the ghetto must be thinking." I could have told them something about that, but I don't think they really wished to know. The "Black ghetto" was so romanticized that, even within the ghetto itself, it always seemed to be somewhere else—an exotic country. The Black outlaw was incessantly idealized, and pampered suburbanites imitated ghetto jive. But when I told people that I had gone to school in Black slums, they would look at me quizzically and say, "You don't sound Black."

As a young college student with a lot of moral fervor and not much judgment, perhaps a bit like my father had been a few decades earlier, I took part in what I thought was a student protest against the Vietnam War. I don't know what, if anything, the protest was actually about, but it was incredibly ill-conceived. The student radicals who led it, with their endless lists of demands and causes, were so unbelievably stupid and brutal that they could not have done a better job of alienating people had they been trying.

I now very seriously wonder whether they *were* trying. It seems plausible enough that some of the protest leaders might have been employed by the FBI or CIA, though I'll probably never know. One evening a crowd of students, on an impulse, decided to go to the house of the University of Chicago President. Rather than participate, I decided to go home, but I learned the next day that they had broken the glass door and almost entered his house. I heard the leader of the protesters say, "What we did grabbed people in the gut, but we didn't go far enough." I regretted having participated in the protests at all, yet I felt duty-bound to stick the damned thing out to the end, not for the sake of any cause but to avoid letting my fellow protesters down or seeming to be a coward. My experience may have been a bit like the trauma of my father after he had been interviewed by the FBI, but, unlike him, I had not passed any point of no return. I would go on to many years of work as a human rights activist in Amnesty International and similar organizations.

For better or worse, my father and Ted Hall lived in a world of enormous intensity, such as most people today can barely imagine. Across the political spectrum, people proclaimed their visions with an enormous moral fervor. They thought that there was some secret key to unlock the understanding of the universe, whether this was Psychoanalysis, Communism, or Evangelical Christianity. Everything was viewed in the perspective of World War II, which seemed to be an epic struggle between good and evil. In an era when everything from art to sex is subjected to enormous trivialization, I often long for that intense engagement. For me, however, the great challenge is largely that of remaining a decent human being, attuned to the natural world and to the needs of others, amid the temptations and distractions that fill everyday life.

The family that I was raised in has probably recovered from the traumas of the 1960s and 1970s as well as could be reasonably expected. My brother stays in the highly regarded Fountain House residence in New York City, where he works in a horticulture program. Over the years, he has become very gentle and calm. My sister is an artist, and her most recent show had good reviews. I have said relatively little about my siblings in order to leave them their own stories, which they may tell, conceal, celebrate, forget, or change as they prefer. My mother died in 2011, surrounded by family and friends, and, as I write this she is still being deeply mourned.

I am a professor, and have published a number of books on animals in legend and literature. My students today do not take life nearly as seriously as the generations of their parents and grandparents did. My own generation, the "baby boomers," was simply a transition, less passionately ideological than that of our parents and more so than our successors. It is amazing how easily nearly everyone has forgotten the utter terror of the Cold War, when everyone constantly worried not only about buildings but entire cities being blown to pieces.

One lesson here may be that spies and terrorists are not so unlike the rest of us after all, but are subject to much the same vanities, aspirations, longings, and frailties. For this reason, I believe it is a big mistake to say that we will never talk or negotiate with sponsors of terrorism. Dialogue generally has some potential to help, even when it is with Nazis, Stalinists, members of the Ku Klux Klan, or agents of some radical Muslim underground. This does not preclude remaining wary or even the continuation of armed hostilities.

My story of intrigue shows, above all, that frustrated spiritual aspirations can drive people to extreme acts including espionage and terrorism. The appeal of the Communist movement was largely that it offered a high drama beyond that of paltry everyday life. It was a forum for grand ambitions, dreams, and, above all, sacrifices. My father and Ted Hall sought in Communism, with its dramatic simplicity, a spirituality that they could not find amid the commercial and technocratic agendas that, in their era and today, dominate American society. That ideology promised them a place in the cosmos and in society, something they were otherwise unable to achieve.

Boria Sax (on the right) with his brother Josh Sax in New York's Central Park, 2011.

Courtesy of the author

But the solution to our problems is not simply to return to some religious orthodoxy or secular tradition, at least not if that is done in an unreflective way. The solution is most especially not the absurd, but absurdly persistent, delusion that war provides a sort of spiritual cleansing by forcing people to live by more exalted values. In the absence of authentic spirituality, people may again sacralize the tools of annihilation, confusing terror with holiness and death with devotion.

Now, a bit older than sixty years, I continually think back on my childhood in Chicago. The wind from Lake Michigan would blend the heat of steel mills, shouting of drunks, fumes of stockyards, smoke of greasy chicken, and perfume of ladies, as it hissed around city blocks. Then snow would descend until all of the odors, noises, and colors had vanished entirely. I sat at the window, remembering the city in all its brutal sensuality, as boots first disfigured the expanse of white.

Photograph by Charles Levy, with permission of the Los Alamos National Laboratory Archives

Notes

1. Joseph Albright and Marcia Kunstel, *Bombshell: The Secret Story of America's Unknown Atomic Spy* (New York: Crown, 1997).
2. Ibid., p. 61.
3. Ibid., *xii.*
4. Boria Sax, "The Boy Who Gave the Bomb Away," *The New York Times Magazine*, 5 October 1997, 12.
5. Albright and Kunstel, 288–289.
6. Robert Conquest, *Harvest of Sorrow* (New York: Oxford University Press, 1987), 331–34. Other estimates of the number killed vary from three million to ten million.
7. James Baldwin, *The Fire Next Time* (New York: Vintage, 1991), 37.
8. Savy reported that he had carried a briefcase full of secret information to the Soviet Consulate. This would not be the usual procedure for spies, who preferred to deliver such materials in places that were less likely to be observed. On the other hand, procedures in espionage are unpredictable, and spies at times deliberately do what they think their adversaries will least expect.
9. Sisela Bok, *Lying: Moral Choice in Public and Private Life* (New York: Vintage, 1999), 18, 28.
10. William L. Laurence, *Dawn over Zero: The Story of the Atomic Bomb* (New York: Knopf, 1946), 273.
11. A note in the archives of the former Soviet Union dated October 2, 1944 states unequivocally that J. Robert Oppenheimer, who headed the scientists at the Manhattan Project, did in fact spy for the Russians. This is reproduced and translated in: Jerrold Schechter and Leona Schechter, *Sacred Secrets: How Soviet Intelligence Operations Changed American History* (Washington, DC: Brassey's, 2002), 198–206, 313–317. This note does not definitively prove that Oppenheimer was a spy, since it is possible that the agent who wrote it was misinformed.
12. Weinstein, Allen, and Alexander Vassiliev. *The Haunted Wood: Soviet Espionage in America.* New York: Modern Library, 2000; 195.

13. Nigel West, *Venona: The Greatest Secret of the Cold War* (New York: HarperCollins, 2000), 142–143. In this document, the true names of the young conspirators were used, but in later ones they were referred to in code.

14. Ibid.

15. "Venona Documents," United States Government http://www.nsa.gov/ public_info/declass/venona/dated.shtml (accessed 29 August 2002).

16. Albright and Kunstel, 143.

17. Allen Weinstein and Alexander Vassiliev, *The Haunted Wood: Soviet Espionage in America, the Stalin Era* (New York: Modern Library, 1999), 209.

18. Luc Santé, "What Secrets Tell," *The New York Times Magazine*, 3 December 2000, 77.

19. Theodore Ziolkowski, *The Sin of Knowledge: Ancient Themes and Modern Variations* (Princeton, NJ: Princeton University Press, 2000), 115.

20. Laurence, 11.

21. Robert Jay Lifton and Greg Mitchell, *Hiroshima in America: A Half Century of Denial* (New York: Avon, 1995), 16.

22. Paul Boyer, *By the Dawn's Early Light: American Thought and Culture at the Dawn of the Atomic Age* (Chapel Hill, NC: University of North Carolina Press, 1994), 266–267.

23. Anonymous, "Atomic Age," *Time Magazine*, 20 August 1945, 29.

24. J. Samuel Walker, "The Decison to Use the Atomic Bomb: A Historigraphical Update," ed. Michael J. Horgan (New York: Cambrige University Press, 1966), 22–24.

25. Boyer, 109–121.

26. Laurence, 11.

27. John Canady, *The Nuclear Muse: Literature, Physics and the First Atomic Bomb* (Madison, WI: University of Wisconsin Press, 2000), 183.

28. Laurence, 223.

29. Saville Sax, *Poetry by Saville Sax* (Chicago: No publisher given, circa 1950). The mimeographed manuscript has no further bibliographical data or pagination.

30. Ibid.

31. Richard Rhodes, "The Myth of Perfect Nuclear Security," *The New York Times*, 24 July 2000, A19. It is possible that Rhodes may be uncritically repeating a claim by Soviet scientists, who did not want to share credit for their atomic bomb with either Americans or spies.

32. Saville Sax, "David, circa 1953." The worst errors in grammar and spelling have been corrected in the quotations from this manuscript. Savy, whose

first language was Yiddish, had not yet mastered written English, and the original contains such errors in almost every line.

33. Kim Philby, "Foreword by Graham Greene," in *My Silent War: The Autobiography of a Spy* (New York: Modern Library, 2002), vii.

34. Ronald Radosh and Joyce Milton, *The Rosenberg File: A Search for Truth* (New York: Reinhart & Wilson, 1989), 42–46.

35. Since then the guilt of the Rosenbergs has been confirmed by the release of the Venona documents in 1995, as well as the testimony of many important figures from Alexander Feklisov, handler of Julius Rosenberg, to former Soviet Premier Nikita Krushchev. Controversies about the trial and execution continue even today. For one thing, Ethel Rosenberg, who died in such a terrifying manner, appears to have had no more than a peripheral role in her husband's espionage. The literature on the Rosenberg case is enormous, but the most comprehensive account of it to date is still probably Radosh and Milton.

36. Albright and Kunstel, 240.

37. Schechter and Schechter, 207.

38. Vladimir Chikov and Gary Kern, "How Stalin Stole the Bomb from the Americans, circa 1998." This unpublished manuscript was supplied to the author by Gary Kern. A version in French has been published under the title *Comment Stalin a volé la bombe aux Américans* (Paris: Robert Laffont, 1999).

39. Christopher Andrew and Vasili Mitrokhin, *The Sword and the Shield: The Mitrokhin Archive and the Secret History of the KGB* (New York: Basic Books, 1999), 147–148.

40. Albright and Kunstel, 177–200.

41. Ralph Blumenthal, "Raid on 'Weird' Commune Here Turns up $30,000 in Fake Bills," *The New York Times*, July 28, 1973, 27.

42. Saville Sax and Sandra Hollander, *Wake the Dragon: A Book on Awareness, Meditation, Centering, Self-Shaping* (Edwardsville, IL: Reality Games Institute, 1975), 7, 48.

43. Sax, *Poetry by Saville Sax*.

44. Alexander Feklisov and Sergei Kostin, *The Man Behind the Rosenbergs* (New York: Enigma, 2001), 13.

Index of Persons